Advance Praise for *Fear and*

"John Kuhn's book is packed with more wisdom than any 10 books that I have read about American education. It is the wisdom born of experience. It is the wisdom of a man who cares about children, families, and community. It is a wisdom that reflects a man with a heart, a brain, a soul, and a connection among them. When I read the manuscript, I thought I would underline the best, most memorable phrases. When I finished, I had so many pages with underlined sentences and bracketed paragraphs that I could not cite them all. I leave that to the fortunate reader of this fine book."

—From the Foreword by **Diane Ravitch**, author of *Reign of Error*

"In *Fear and Learning in America*, John Kuhn weaves together stories from his life as a teacher and missionary with tales from history (the Panama Canal, Japanese internment during World War II, and Pizarro's slaughter of the Incas, for example). The result is a fresh way of thinking about schools and educational policy. Refuting *A Nation at Risk*, Mr. Kuhn warns, persuasively, of 'a rising tide of inequality.' His message, artfully delivered in this important book, should be heeded."

—**John Merrow**, education correspondent, PBS NewsHour; president, Learning Matters, Inc.

"Kuhn is a superb educator and his valuable book effectively dissects the myths about today's high-stakes testing environment and the worsening conditions under which educators are expected to make miracles every day, or else. His cogent arguments against such policies demonstrate what is really important and should inform the debate about public education."

—**Randi Weingarten**, president, American Federation of Teachers

"This book is a brilliantly clear defense of public education as our nation's most valuable asset. In *Fear and Learning in America*, John Kuhn fearlessly names the fact that today's education reformers, like the renowned emperor, wear no clothes. Through stories and elegant prose, he dissects claims and strategies of the missionaries, politicians, and corporations who hawk psychometric solutions to manufactured problems as they scapegoat teachers, families, and kids, all while avoiding the real problem of escalating inequality."

—**Christine Sleeter**, professor emerita, California State University Monterey Bay

"At a time when the wisdom and perspective of educators is more needed than ever, John Kuhn offers his in a voice that is at turns angry, compassionate, and inspired. With a mixture of personal and professional reflections, Kuhn outlines the ways in which our current efforts to improve public schooling have missed the mark, while celebrating the ongoing work of educators to create respectful, democratic environments that can help children learn and grow."

—**Sam Chaltain**, writer and education activist

"As a teacher, there's not much I appreciate more than courageous administrators willing to speak out against the insanity and injustice of the current 'reform' movement. With this book, John Kuhn shows once again that he is one of the most fearless."

—**Gregory Michie**, bestselling author of *Holler If You Hear Me, Second Edition*; 7th/8th-grade teacher, Chicago Public Schools

"Superintendent John Kuhn has written a masterpiece filled with scholarship, science, and stories about real students and real schools. He, like his fellow Texan, Diane Ravitch (*Reign of Error: The Hoax of Privatization*) are calling the charlatans out. From the miracle schools snake-oil salesmen, to the politicians using cribbed legislation from ALEC, Kuhn is unafraid to challenge the 'status quo' of educational inequity. He is at his best when he shares the stories about his own students and what he was and was not able to do. Texas is lucky to have an educator of his stature."

—**Karen G. J. Lewis**, president, Chicago Teachers Union

"Through compellingly written personal narrative, vignettes, historical examples, and research, John Kuhn's *Fear and Learning in America* tells the story of how a teacher-turned-superintendent transformed into an activist against corporate education reform in Texas and around the nation. This is an important story for all those interested in working towards a more just system of public education."

—**Wayne Au**, associate professor,
University of Washington, Bothell; editor, *Rethinking Schools*.

THE TEACHING FOR SOCIAL JUSTICE SERIES

William Ayers—*Series Editor*
Therese Quinn—*Associate Series Editor*
Editorial Board: Hal Adams, Barbara Bowman, Lisa Delpit, Michelle Fine, Maxine Greene,
Caroline Heller, Annette Henry, Asa Hilliard, Rashid Khalidi, Gloria Ladson-Billings, Charles Payne,
Mark Perry, Luis Rodriguez, Jonathan Silin, William Watkins

Fear and Learning in America

Bad Data, Good Teachers,
and the Attack on Public Education

✪ ✪ ✪

JOHN KUHN

Foreword by **Diane Ravitch**

Teachers College, Columbia University
New York and London

Published by Teachers College Press, 1234 Amsterdam Avenue, New York, NY 10027

Library of Congress Cataloging-in-Publication Data

Kuhn, John, author.
    Fear and learning in America : Bad data, good teachers, and the attack on
    public education / John Kuhn.
        p. cm. — (Teaching for social justice series)
    Includes bibliographical references and index.
    ISBN 978-0-8077-5572-3 (pbk. : alk. paper)
    ISBN 978-0-8077-7277-5 (e-book)
        1. Public schools—United States. 2. Educational change—United States.
    3. Education—Standards—United States. 4. Educational equalization—
    United States. I. Title.
    LA217.2.K84 2014
    371.010973—dc23   2013043346

ISBN 978-0-8077-5572-3 (paper)
eISBN 978-0-8077-7277-5

Printed on acid-free paper
Manufactured in the United States of America

21   20   19   18   17   16   15   14   8   7   6   5   4   3   2   1

The educational foundations of our society are presently being eroded by a rising tide of mediocrity that threatens our very future as a Nation and a people.

—*A Nation at Risk*, 1983

Pray, do come and help me; the Wolf is killing the sheep.

—"The Boy Who Cried Wolf," Aesop

Contents

✪ ✪ ✪

Foreword

I HAD NEVER HEARD OF John Kuhn until one day in 2011 when I received an email from him. It contained an eloquent protest against the budget cuts planned by the Governor of the State of Texas. Being a fellow Texan, though long removed from my native state, I immediately put Mr. Kuhn in touch with Valerie Strauss of the *Washington Post*, who published it on her daily blog, The Answer Sheet. With that articulate defense of his district, John Kuhn became a star among those of us who were increasingly concerned that education "reform" had turned into an assault against education itself.

That summer, John Kuhn was a featured speaker at the national Save Our Schools rally, where he brought the crowd of thousands to its feet, cheering his message of alarm, hope, and defiance. I met him yet again when he addressed the Save Texas Schools march in Austin in 2013.

What was so striking about John was that he wasn't boasting that he knew how to get test scores higher than anyone else. He wasn't claiming that he had found the magic elixir to solve the problems of the schools. What I remember was that he spoke about the children in his schools. He said, "Send me your children who can't speak English. Send me your children with disabilities. I want them all. I will help them all." Those may not have been his exact words, but that was his message. If not an elixir, his words were like a stream of cool clear water in the middle of a desert. He spoke from the heart. He spoke the words of a teacher, a man who really did put children first.

When I started reading his book, I braced myself for the usual turgid prose that all school officials have mastered. But that was not what I found. I found the stories and memories of a man who made a decision to devote his life to education. I found myself unable to skim. I read every word. I found myself listening to the wisdom of a man who speaks directly and without artifice. Unlike some superintendents who have mastered the art of blandness—the art of never offending anyone who might take issue with something he said—John Kuhn speaks from the heart. Some of his stories are heart-warming. Some are heart-breaking. I was moved by the accounts of the young men who decided they had to drop out of high school because they couldn't pass the math test. They had what it takes to be good citizens, but they just couldn't pass that test no matter how many times they tried. The legislature made the rules, Kuhn had to abide by them, and the lives of these two fine young men were blighted.

As I read his stories of the injustices perpetrated on children by an unfeeling and unwise system, I imagined the people in Austin making the laws. They didn't see the children. They didn't look into their eyes. They didn't see the hurt. They didn't see the lost potential. John Kuhn did.

At one point, I thought I would write this Foreword by quoting some of his most memorable lines. But there are so many that I will quote just a few to give you some idea of this man and how he thinks. He notes at the outset that he felt "compelled to join the band of fearless educators who have noticed a swarm of well-meaning dabblers and malevolent vandals tearing away at the foundations of American public education in broad daylight." He writes that "a ceaseless PR campaign dedicated to the devaluation of our public school system led by corporate lobbyists and billionaire anti-unionists should give us all pause. The crusade to cheapen this public trust is breathtaking for its audacity and its tenacity. More breathtaking still: the credulity of a media that refuses to examine the motives of public schools' suspiciously eager condemners, and the inexplicable sympathies of both political parties as they grease the skids for the hostile takeover."

John Kuhn is a superintendent with the heart of a teacher. He writes, "I learned to admire teachers after being in the trenches with them. We stood up for academics and character while the wider culture around us lauded vulgarity. We stood up for kids who were bullied and we reached out to those isolated because they were different. . . . Each of us stood for the good and the noble and the just in ways that no one but the kids themselves would ever see. We were workaday patriots, without guns or parades. We just did the work, took the lumps, and satisfied ourselves with the knowledge that our standing in the middle class was relatively secure. We would never be rich, it was true, but we would also never be poor." The public would never understand how hard it was to be a teacher, but at least, until the last decade, when corporate elites and think tank experts launched an unprecedented era of teacher-bashing, teachers were respected. Kuhn was baffled and disgusted when the teacher-bashing began. He can even pinpoint the specific television program that made him aware of it (reported by John Stossel), and he recoiled in disgust, knowing that "the only real sin of teachers is being paid with tax receipts that come from people who don't particularly want to pay taxes."

Superintendent Kuhn understands a basic fact about American schools that has thus far eluded the President of the United States, the Secretary of Education, governors, and legislatures: "The dollar value of residential properties in a school district . . . [is] a far bigger determinant of a school's rating than teacher quality." Rich districts have greater resources and better results. Poor districts have fewer resources, their students have higher needs, and the test scores are lower. This is not "blaming the victim." This is telling the unvarnished truth.

John Kuhn's book is packed with more wisdom than any 10 books that I have read about American education. It is the wisdom born of experience. It is the wisdom of a man who cares about children, families, and community. It is a wisdom that reflects a man with a heart, a brain, a soul, and a connection among them.

When I read the manuscript, I thought I would underline the best, most memorable phrases. When I finished, I had so many pages with underlined sentences and bracketed paragraphs that I could not cite them all. I leave that to the fortunate reader of this fine book.

—Diane Ravitch

✪ ✪ ✪

Introduction

"THE ONLY THING A superintendent needs to know is how to count to four." So goes a saying among school leaders in Texas, the meaning of which is fairly obvious: If you serve at the pleasure of seven board members, as long as four of them are on your side, everything else is pretty simple. As soon as four or more of the seven decide they don't want you around, you're done for.

It is with full awareness of the wisdom of this dictum that I sit down to write.

Fear and Learning in America started, for all intents and purposes, with *A Nation at Risk* (1983). A clumsy slap at the institution of public education, the report's hyperbole and hysterics led us down a winding path to a place, today, of real risk: the end of public education altogether. Nothing in America's glorious history has been as democratizing as public education for minority students and female students and students with special needs. If it weren't for public schools, there would have been no integration. If it weren't for public schools, there would have been no Title IX. If it weren't for public schools, there would have been no Individuals with Disabilities Education Act.

Writing about education policy is a dangerous proposition for any practicing educator, but especially for a school superintendent. All I have to do to wreck my happy stay in my current position is to offend enough people. By recording in black and white for all posterity any opinion I may have about the intersection of education and politics, I run the risk of staking out a position that affronts some fundamental belief of my board member bosses, their bosses, their spouses, their parents, or the people they play golf or go shopping with.

Simply put, smart superintendents don't poke at hornets' nests with sticks.

Speaking out (about anything, really) has little upside for educators, and lots of potential downside. First, teachers aren't usually wealthy. Most are middle-class working stiffs with meager savings who can't afford to miss a paycheck or two while they search for another job. (As a superintendent, I certainly earn more than I did as a teacher, but I'm not well-off enough that I don't need next month's paycheck.) Secondly, we serve communities whose inhabitants possess diverse political beliefs; virtually any position we embrace will be anathema to some neighbor whose tax dollars fund our paychecks. It might be safe to campaign on behalf of puppies and ice cream, but when it comes to divisive issues like school funding, equity, taxation, school choice—any issue about which people disagree and are passionate—the best thing for an educator to do is keep his or her mouth shut and just teach.

Smart educators are all things to all people.

Maybe this explains why so many American educators have watched passively as a hit parade of ill-conceived education policies captured the attention of our nation's decisionmakers and were enshrined in our federal and state law books. We and our students were as meek as lambs led to a standardized slaughter.

It seems important in light of the test-punish-and-churn horrors that my prior reticence has wrought for my students (and my own children) to accept the proposition that contending for dangerous truths is integral to the job of the modern American educator. When teachers, principals, superintendents, and school board members stand alongside students and parents to insist on a place at the table, our country will be well on its way to a more balanced, healthy, effective, and beneficial system of education policy development, and that will be good for children and for the nation's future. The wholesale harms of policycrafters, inadvertent as they may be, are often more clearly seen by the practitioners and the parents who deal with the fallout from implementation. Feedback from the front lines is vital, even if it is at times unwelcome.

That is not to suggest that educators should risk their employment by speaking out cavalierly against every policy with which they disagree. Instead, educators should seek safe platforms for the expression of their legitimate professional concerns. Anonymous means of responding to the latest educational fad are easy to find in the Internet age, and there's strength in numbers through educator associations and grassroots groups that have sprung up in recent years to defend the ideals of public education. Armies of educators and their supporters can wage philosophical battles on Twitter and Facebook and in the comments sections of online articles about education, often using pseudonyms for their own professional protection.

Writing this book and, simultaneously, a complementary book called *Test-and-Punish* (Park Place Publications) might well be a mistake. Nonetheless, I feel compelled to join the band of fearless educators who have noticed a swarm of well-meaning dabblers and malevolent vandals tearing away at the foundations of American public education in broad daylight.

I write this book to warn that the folks spending their leisure time declaring the American public school system an utter failure have an embarrassing number of conflicting interests and ulterior motives. Unabashed, they tenaciously peddle their remarkably consistent message: *Schools are bad. Unions are the problem. The free market is the solution.* This book focuses on the first plank of that triune assurance.

Maybe the teachers I know and respect are truly as bad as they imply and I'm too biased to see it. Or maybe I've just been remarkably lucky in my career and have largely avoided the bad teachers that we are constantly assured fill our schools to overflowing.

Or maybe they're misleading us.

In a young century already noted for brazen corporate malfeasance in fields ranging from energy to mortgage finance to banking to insurance, a ceaseless PR campaign dedicated to the devaluation of our public school system led by corporate lobbyists and billion-aire anti-unionists should give us all pause. The crusade to cheapen this public trust is breathtaking for its audacity and its tenacity. More breathtaking still: the credulity of a media that refuses to examine the motives of public schools' suspiciously eager condemners, and the inexplicable sympathies of both political parties as they grease the skids for the hostile takeover.

It is because I'm quite close to three little people whom I hope will graduate from public schools, and because I assume that I'll have grandkids in public schools someday (if such schools still exist) that I write this book.

✪ ONE ✪

An Unlikely Activist

WHEN I WAS YOUNG AND FIT, I spent 2 years in Peru. I fell in love with the people and the culture, but more than that, I fell in love with a pretty college girl named Noelia.

Before I met Noelia, a teacher was the last thing I wanted to be. I had three sisters who either were or were on their way to becoming teachers. Not me.

My future was in the written word. In fact, I would have become a sportswriter if not for an academic scholarship to Tarleton State University.

Tarleton is a great institution and I'm still a fan. But in 1991 TSU didn't offer a major in journalism. So English it was, with a teaching certification on the side to placate my mom. Throw in a history minor, and I was set for a career in Lone Star public education. *Stamping out ignorance*, as a colleague used to say.

But I was determined that wasn't going to happen.

After graduation I took a job as a long-term sub while I waited to begin a 2-year stint in the Southern Baptist version of the Peace Corps. I taught well, I suppose, but 2 months of grading stacks of badly written papers confirmed what I already knew: Teaching wasn't for me. Peru would give me time to plan for another career.

For 2 years in the Andes, I daydreamed about returning home and finding some amazing job that wasn't teaching.

But Noelia's long hair was as black as coal, and it fell down onto her shoulders in a mess of careless beauty. She was 19. I had never heard a name as pretty as hers. I pestered her for a photo together;

later, our first date was to a pizza place. We drank Inca Kola and I stared at her a little too much.

A few months before my Peru gig was up, I made a decision. I would ask her to marry me. If she said yes, I'd need a job as soon as I got home.

Back then, teaching jobs weren't as scarce as they've become. And teachers weren't as generally dumped on. I wasn't thrilled about the thought of teaching snarky teenagers for the rest of my life, but all I could really think about in those days was the honeymoon.

Long story short, she said yes one night at Huanchaco Beach.

I came home and tried out the now-hallowed private sector, and I began saving up for the wedding. I was shipping manager at a window factory.

I tried to satisfy myself with this occupation. I had just spent 2 years weighing babies with wind-burned cheeks on scales I hung from tree branches, building churches out of mud bricks, and drilling water wells in villages where people drank out of streams and cisterns. I couldn't seem to find fulfillment making sure 50 windows were shipped to the right place and we got the best deal on freight.

My sister called one day and told me the Spanish teacher at her school was leaving. I spoke Spanish and had a teaching degree: Was I interested?

The wedding was a month away. The factory was killing me. I interviewed.

Teaching Spanish was the right fit. Parents and older teachers told me I was good. I felt good. I enjoyed the kids, especially the smart alecks and the Spanish speakers and the head bangers. I think they enjoyed me too, and together we mostly enjoyed the subject I taught. During the first semester, I decided this is what I would do with my life. My friends would make more money, but I didn't care. I only needed my wife and our future.

To make ends meet I had to take a side job as a youth minister one month into my new career. In fact, between youth ministry, bus routes, fireworks stands, and working weekends and summers for Upward Bound, I never *only* taught. It wasn't feasible, not even with no kids and a house we bought for $10,000. Our first dinner table was a folding card table. Our first television set came out of a stranger's trash bin. He said it didn't work, but we got six months' use out of that TV.

Back then, I never dreamed teachers would one day be considered greedy.

We made it. We even bought a cell phone and, eventually, paid cash for a used Dodge Shadow. I got a free Jack Russell Terrier along the way, and I got up every morning and taught teenagers Spanish, good study habits, pride in America and Texas and their small hometown, and the importance of getting an education. I tried to be a role model. I didn't drink, I didn't smoke, and I went to church every Sunday.

I was surrounded by middle-class men and women who were as decent and fallible as people come. I learned that older teachers in small-town Texas love grandkids and travel more than anything else. And teachers young and old tend to invest themselves authentically in family, church, and community.

I learned to admire teachers after being in the trenches with them. We stood up for academics and character while the wider culture around us lauded vulgarity. We stood up for kids who were bullied and we reached out to those isolated because they were different. We reported child abuse. Each of us in our own way fought for the future well-being of our society in a million seemingly inconsequential interactions with blossoming adults; each of us stood for the good and the noble and the just in ways that no one but the kids themselves would ever see. We were workaday patriots, without guns or parades. We just did the work, took the lumps, and satisfied ourselves with the knowledge that our standing in the middle class was relatively secure. We would never be rich, it was true, but we would also never be poor.

It's a tough job, but if I can speak for the teachers I've known, I'd say we felt every sacrifice was worth it because our communities had our backs. The esteem for us that I believed was out there always meant as much to me as the paycheck.

A lot has changed since 1997.

"Stupid in America"

The first indication I got that teacher-bashing was going mainstream came when I saw a John Stossel report called "Stupid in America" on *20/20*. Stossel called for school choice, noting that when the government had a monopoly on telephone service we all had black phones and high phone bills (Stossel, 2006a, p. 4). He described teachers who committed criminal sexual acts and couldn't be fired in New York City; he quoted the head of the New York City school system complaining about the teachers' union protecting bad teachers; he noted that school funding in the United States had increased without a commensurate improvement in test scores; and he stated that, depending on their zip codes, some American children were trapped in failing schools with no recourse (Stossel, 2006a, 2006b). Nothing was said, of course, about public schools that were working well. His report was a sterling example of confirmation bias but a poor example of journalism. He wasn't pursuing truth; he was laying on a sales pitch.

At that time, I was a card-carrying member of the religious right. I had spent 4 years as a college commuter flipping my radio back and forth between Rush Limbaugh and contemporary Christian music on KLTY, where music was "safe for the whole family."

I loved John Stossel in those days. We were on the same team. When he turned his guns on teachers, I was confused. I had heartily agreed with him so many times. In fact, I saw him as one of the few redeeming voices in the "liberal media." When he started talking about how great teachers had it, and how it was a popular myth that they were underpaid—even as my wife and I had struggled to afford a Spartan lifestyle—I decided he must in truth be a closet liberal or something. How else could he be so wrong?

The Sunday after John Stossel's attack, my three teacher sisters and I discussed the report on the breezy patio behind my parents' house. The sense of betrayal was palpable. We didn't feel underworked or overpaid. I had never seen a rubber room.

That was a tipping point. John Stossel was the first name on a list of people I wouldn't take at face value anymore. He had lied by gross omission about me and my salt-of-the-earth colleagues. He had portrayed us all as takers instead of givers, had declared us all guilty by highlighting the worst and concealing the best among us, a ruse anyone could pull about any occupation at any time. Even journalism.

The scales fell from my eyes. How many times had I nodded along as angry friends and radio hosts bashed this people group or that people group, highlighting their most noteworthy failures and glossing over everything else?

The image so carefully cultivated for me by Rush Limbaugh and others that conservatives were about small town values and liberals were for anything-goes urban hedonism and rampant welfare waste was suddenly upended. With one primetime news broadcast, teachers were cast as American malefactors alongside socialists, homosexuals, welfare moms, and intravenous drug users, and I lost my faith in the script.

Canary in the Mine

Sadly, John Stossel wasn't an outlier in 2006. He was a big, mustachioed canary in the mine presaging the world we live in today. On the heels of his pioneering work of primetime teacher-bashing would come a relentless flurry of attacks on the dignity and worth of teachers.

The fact is that teachers are an important part of the backbone of small towns like the ones that have been my stomping grounds. With few exceptions, they are the picture of unassuming decency. They keep their yards mowed and their houses painted. To John Stossel and his ideological brethren, they have somehow become the enemy, but not because they're lazy or ineffective, because they're not. And it's not because they're overpaid: As of this writing, Texas's starting teacher wage is just under $30,000 (and most Texas teachers pay hundreds per month toward health insurance and retirement). They drive Hyundais, as Jon Stewart has hilariously noted. Despite the rhetoric listing their supposed crimes, the only real sin of teachers is being paid with tax receipts that come from people who don't particularly want to pay taxes.

On a back-to-school night as a young principal, I stood in front of a crowd of 300 parents and students and asked my staff to join me onstage. I wanted my community to understand what kinds of people were teaching their kids. I wanted to counteract the poison that had been injected into the national discourse about public education.

"Teachers, raise your hand if you're a military veteran," I said. Several hands went up among my teachers. Polite applause came from the crowd.

"Raise your hand if you've ever taught Sunday school." Applause.

"If you've ever coached Little League."

"If you've ever volunteered with scouts."

"If you've worked elections."

"If you're a blood donor."

"If you've helped in a homeless shelter, a clothes closet, a soup kitchen, or a food pantry."

"Raise your hand if you've ever been a volunteer firefighter."

Time and again, an audience of public school parents and their fresh-faced kids clapped for the teachers. And the teachers beamed. It became apparent to me there in the glare of the stage lights that these people—as diverse in age and gender and ethnicity as the audience staring up at them, but all sharing the title of "teacher"—had not been extolled enough. They hadn't sought appreciation; they had only tried to be upstanding members of society. They would never ask for a pat on the back from their neighbors. But I could see that it did them immeasurable good. They needed it. And in my view then and now, they deserved it.

The Big Bad Test

As a student I enjoyed standardized tests. I figured out that "percentile" meant I was better than that percentage of American children, and I lived for the 99th percentile.

Fast-forward a few years. As a young schoolteacher, I was all for Texas's TAAS test. My only complaint was that I had to actually administer it, and it seemed like a big fat waste of my valuable time. Other than that, I had no qualms. As a Spanish teacher, I wasn't under the microscope for my kids' scores, so I didn't know what all the math, reading, science, and social studies teachers were whining about.

Texas schools were labeled based on student test scores. The labels were Exemplary, Recognized, Acceptable, and Unacceptable. I occasionally heard people criticize the testing that drove the system, but the ready response I had in mind was, "You don't want a doctor operating on you unless they've passed a medical exam, do you?"

After a few years of teaching, though, I noticed something extremely predictable about the test-based accountability system. Year after year, I watched as school districts filled with tracts of brick homes got labeled Exemplary while those full of older frame homes got labeled Recognized or (shudder) Acceptable. And districts with federally subsidized apartment complexes? They were lucky if they got Acceptable.

The school accountability competition wasn't really a contest at all. It was more like a children's tale, with schools starring as the Three Little Pigs and the test as the Big Bad Wolf. The schools that had bricks did well; the schools that had straw did poorly.

Not only were schools in wealthier towns invariably rated a notch higher than schools in middle-class towns, but there was also this: When the new, more rigorous Texas Assessment of Knowledge and Skills (TAKS) test was introduced and knocked everyone back a peg or two, the wealthy burgs achieved nirvana again fairly quickly. The middle-class towns reached the Exemplary level a year or 2 later, and then finally lagging at the back of the pack came the districts full of poor kids.

Poverty wasn't an excuse; it was an ironclad guarantee.

In local newspapers and on the 10 o'clock news, our system told teachers and kids in bedroom communities, "You're the best." And the kids who were born in the zip codes where none of our state leaders would dare raise their children were destined to hear, relentlessly, "You're not good enough."

The message was never "You're low-resourced," even though it was true. The disparate levels of educational funding made available to Texas communities were never talked about openly, nor were they published in handy spreadsheets or posted online by the state and disseminated to news organizations, unlike the test-based accountability labels. When citizens and reporters wanted to know about schools, Texas officials handed out microscopes for studying test-based outcomes, but they gave out blindfolds for looking at funding inputs.

In my rural school, I had taught well-off kids alongside distressingly poor kids, and, as most people would expect, I found that well-off kids were far easier to get across the standardized testing finish line. Their parents were more responsive if you called about an assignment not turned in. The students were more likely to study and more likely to get punished at home for academic shenanigans like cheating or not completing assignments. It made sense to me even back then that the quickest and easiest way to win the Super Bowl of school accountability was to draft the best team you could. If poor parents with disadvantages like a paucity of books in the home, insufficient dollars for Sylvan, night jobs keeping them from monitoring homework, and sometimes frequent moves can't afford to live in your district, your school is halfway to its goal.

The dollar value of residential properties in a school district, then, was a far bigger determinant of a school's rating than teacher quality. And that's not even mentioning the school-funding differences that went along with those differences in property value.

But from the beginning of test-based accountability in Texas, the state was content to pretend school accountability was an objective measure of the quality of the teachers in a school.

Deliberate Inequity

The year 2006 found Texas in a quandary. A state Supreme Court decision had held the prior school-funding law to be unconstitutional, and leadership wanted to satisfy the court and at the same time provide tax-averse Texans with relief from rising property levies. School districts depended on property taxes for their very survival, however. In the end, the state compressed property taxes by one-third and made up for districts' losses by tweaking a business margins tax. School officials were assured that the margins tax would cover the lost property tax revenue. A raise for teachers only sweetened the deal.

Key to the new school funding setup was a mechanism called "target revenue." Essentially, schools would be locked into a per-pupil[1] revenue level based on the higher point of their funding from either 2005 or 2006. If a depression in property values were to hit a school district or a major employer packed up and left town, the school wouldn't take a funding hit. Instead, the state would step in and cover the lost revenue to keep it at its target level. On the flip side, schools would no longer see a windfall if a giant new business set up shop in the district.

After looking at the bill and running the numbers, state comptroller Carole Keeton Strayhorn in 2006 contended that the margins tax wouldn't generate what lawmakers said it would. Strayhorn reported that Texas would find its school-funding liabilities severely outpacing its available resources under the new law, leading to a $23 billion shortfall in 5 years. She called it the "largest hot check in Texas history" (Scharrer, 2011). Governor Rick Perry and many others dismissed the comptroller's concerns as political theater, however, noting that Strayhorn had declared she was running against Perry in the next gubernatorial election.

Besides questions about the math, the bill had another flaw: Target revenues in property-poor districts were up to thousands of dollars less per pupil than in property-wealthy districts. Advocates for the state assured the Supreme Court of their intentions to pursue equitable school funding by raising the lower-funded target revenues gradually over the next few years. Importantly, however, nothing was written in the statute that would require this.

State Senator Florence Shapiro had been a key architect of Texas's notably inequitable school-funding system—a system that had educationally benefited the children in her well-off voting district far more than it had benefited children educated in poorer Lone Star climes. During negotiations in a committee over one school finance bill, Shapiro led a walkout of senators because the chair of the committee wouldn't let her "scrap the education bill" over her op-position to a change that "would increase the amount of money poor schools are guaranteed from the state." Shapiro's explanation for her walkout was that the bill, as changed, "takes that money from all the schoolchildren and only gives it to some of the schoolchildren. I'm opposed to that" (Austin & Castro, 2006). And Shapiro wasn't alone. Many of Texas's elected officials were primarily dedicated to serv-ing the needs of their constituents when it came to divvying up the state's education dollars.

I still remember the meeting in my superintendent's office when he first explained the new target revenue system to me. The highest-funded school in Texas had a target of over $13,000 per student. Our school district was pegged at $4,747.

I couldn't wrap my head around the idea that a group of elected officials would write into statute that schools should be funded at different fixed levels but then measured against identical perfor-mance standards. This wasn't an accident of the law; it was deliber-ate. When I explained this system to my teachers in our next faculty meeting, many didn't believe me.

The state was "picking winners and losers by the way we fund them," Representative Scott Hochberg would later declare (Smith, 2012b). Sadly, Representative Hochberg came to this realization af-ter learners in my then-district had been clobbered for 6 years by a policy of austerity for them and luxury for their neighbors—a policy that, during just over half a decade, permitted school districts just next door to rack up millions for computers, salaries, and field trips that my students would never see.

I was incensed for my students who were shortchanged educa-tional experiences. I was incensed for my teachers who were short-changed on their paychecks. I was incensed for me: My reputation was on the line if I couldn't figure out how to overcome neighboring schools' fiscal head start.

As if deliberate inequity weren't bad enough, the comptroller was proved right about the margins tax. It indeed underperformed as she had foreseen, and then the Great Recession hit on top of that. The well-meaning government in Austin was never able to follow through on its promise to raise the bottommost target revenues. For well over half a decade, grossly inequitable funding levels stayed frozen. Texas had created a system that guaranteed comparatively underfunded, and, by virtue, comparatively underperforming schools.

The rural high school where I was principal in those days had a poorer and harder-to-educate student body than most of the high-flying suburban schools to our east; we also had less money with which to do the job. But the state's required outcomes on standardized tests didn't bend for hard-luck cases. In order to receive the coveted Exemplary label, a school funded at $4,000 per pupil had to achieve the same standardized test passing rates as a $10,000-per-pupil school. Not fair? Tough luck. If rough-and-tumble kids in the sticks couldn't make the grade with their lower-paid teachers, older computers, and sparser libraries, there was no asterisk in the local paper explaining the education dollar disadvantage they faced at the outset. The only thing the paper would publish would be the one- or two-word label the state handed out to schools based on test scores, no context included. Community members at the local level were left to assume that a lower-ranking school in the state's hierarchy of accountability was simply a less competent institution, full of less competent people. The state did nothing to disavow Lone Star citizens of the notion that school accountability was a fair race; it did nothing to inform them that large-scale funding differences were at play.

When it came to educational accountability, our leaders were content not to lead, but to mislead.

I entered a period of abiding bitterness. I had been treated unfairly, and so had my students, my parents, and my teachers. Even local homeowners were harmed; their property values were adversely affected by school ratings that they assumed were objective and fair.

In my mind, my high school had been set up to fail. I hated the backstabbers who created this system with every fiber of my being each time I pulled up to the front of my school building and saw the brick façade where an "Exemplary" banner would never hang. I wasn't unethical enough to cheat to attain that status, and I wasn't smart enough to overcome the resource disadvantages my students and teachers inherited from a callous state legislature.

The fight for inequity apparently had its benefits, for some. Thanks to the efforts of Texas legislators, the children of the state's nicest suburbs had a guarantee written in law that they would continue to have access to better, higher-funded public schools than the children in most Texas localities. For many of us having to look our students in the eye each day, funding inequity was a wound that wouldn't heal.

The Alamo Letters

February 2011 found Texas public school administrators—especially superintendents, among whose number I had counted myself since the previous August—extremely strung out. The Tea Party–infused state House of Representatives had presented a biennial budget that included $10 billion in cuts from public education. Alarm bells were sounding in school district central offices statewide as we pored over our employee lists and tried to figure out who we would have to let go. State officials blamed the economy and steadfastly refused to acknowledge the role of the inadequate 2006 margins tax substitution. Political special interest groups busily argued that schools had plenty of money, if they would just stop wasting so much on administrative fluff.

At the same time, Texas was moving full steam ahead toward implementation of a new school accountability system and a new testing system. The tests would be called the State of Texas Assessments of Academic Readiness (STAAR), and they would be far more rigorous, would cost more (approaching an astounding $100 million per year), and would eat up more learning days for state testing than ever before. The new system would allow any student to retest anytime for any reason, and the secondary STAAR end-of-course tests would count as 15% of high school course grades.

February 2011 also found me sitting in the conference room of an Austin hotel with maybe 400 other school administrators.

I don't remember who the first speakers were. I'm sure they gave us thought-provoking and valuable information.

But I remember clearly who batted clean-up. It was a state legislator who had led the charge to develop the new, more rigorous

STAAR test and who had also fought to enact the simultaneous budget cuts that were glaring down at Texas educators and their charges.

Over the years, this legislator's name had been attached to one bill after another that expanded test-based accountability's role, its cost, and its draconian intensity. The well-resourced schools in her voting district tended to do well on these tests and typically got top-notch ratings on the systems she championed. Real estate prices in her district benefited from the vinyl "Exemplary!" banners that the state's vaunted sorting scheme helped hang from the eaves of its gleaming schools.

Legislators' support for school labeling, in retrospect, was really support for a faux meritocracy at the public school level, a neoliberal monstrosity that had the effect of subverting opportunity for the unwashed masses in the slums and the sticks, and ensuring it for the children of suburbanites. Before the sorting systems were implemented, only better pay, nicer facilities, and smaller classes drove good teachers toward the suburbs where they were less needed. Thanks to that day's speaker and her friends, though, low-income schools were soon able to add public shame and state-assigned epithets alongside lower salaries and harder work as employment draws on their job fair slide presentations.

In 2011, with the state having stubbornly failed to address inequity in the 5 years since the last funding lawsuit and with a gargantuan shortfall looming, advocacy groups like Austin's Equity Center began urging state lawmakers to take the billions of dollars in coming cuts primarily from higher-funded districts.

That's when the speaker before us stepped in. She argued stridently that funding cuts should hit all schools equally, including the poor ones. She and some of her colleagues essentially fought to preserve funding gaps between high-funded and low-funded schools. In debate during the crafting of a funding bill, she explained her opposition to strategic, equity-enhancing cuts by saying, "This is not an equity bill. This is a bill dealing with cuts in the system" ("Texas won't," 2011). To his credit, a fellow senator named Kel Seliger (who represented a lower-funded district) disagreed. "When we talk about the provision of education to children," he said, "equity is always an issue" ("Texas won't," 2011).

It wasn't a good thing for me to be in the audience listening to the senator's speech that day. I should have excused myself.

She started with platitudes: how great it was to be invited; how much she appreciated us for the hard work we did.

There just wasn't any money, she told us, and this was a really bad recession. She made no mention of the hot check she and her friends had signed a few years earlier. My blood warmed. We would all have to sacrifice, unfortunately. But education is vitally important, she assured us, and we must continue to make progress and hold our schools accountable. For that reason, the great new test—STAAR—would be non-negotiable.

Non-negotiable.

My blood boiled.

We're broke, but no matter what we'll be spending $500 million on tests from Pearson, Inc. over the next 5 years? Even while cutting billions in school funding?

The senator opened up for questions and answers after her speech, which was brave. She probably shouldn't have. I went to the microphone and told her that I was eliminating nine positions out of 64 in my small district.

"Do you have a question?" she asked.

"How many employees do you think Pearson is laying off right now?" I replied.

"I don't have any idea," she said.

"You're saving the test but not the teachers," I replied.

Several other people hammered her with their questions. An elementary principal from San Antonio related how frequently her problem students withdrew to local charter schools only to come sheepishly back to the public school a week or two later when the charter schools kicked them out for misbehaving.

"Does that happen?" the senator asked, aghast.

"All the time," the principal said.

"I was not aware of that," the speaker replied. "Write that down," she told her assistant.

And so it went. Dozens of people spoke. Two or three thanked the legislator for her work on behalf of the children. The rest gave her hardball questions.

When the conflagration was over, I went to the hotel restaurant and sat by myself, mad at the world. In my spare time in those days, I had been working on a book that I wanted to call *Texas Tough Guys.* I had written about my favorites, the heroes of Gonzales, Texas, who made a flag that said "Come and Take It" when Santa Anna tried to confiscate the town's only cannon. And I had written about the men who died in the Alamo, none braver than Colonel William Barret Travis.

I felt a little besieged myself that night. I pulled out my phone and looked up a document I had read many times before: Travis's letter to a rebellious state's leaders pleading for help as his enemies surrounded him.

The Alamo Letter

Commandancy of the Alamo
Bexar, Fby. 24th, 1836
To the People of Texas & all Americans in the world

I am besieged by a thousand or more of the Mexicans under Santa Anna. I have sustained a continual bombardment & cannonade for 24 hours & have not lost a man. The enemy has demanded a surrender at discretion, otherwise the garrison are to be put to the sword if the fort is taken. I have answered the demand with a cannon shot, and our flag still waves proudly from the walls. *I shall never surrender nor retreat.*

Then, I call on you in the name of Liberty, of patriotism, & of everything dear to the American character, to come to our aid with all dispatch. The enemy is receiving reinforcements daily & will no doubt increase to three or four thousand in four or five days. If this call is neglected, I am determined to sustain myself as long as possible & die like a soldier who

never forgets what is due to his own honor & that of his
country.

Victory or Death
William Barret Travis
Lt. Col. Comdt.

P.S. The Lord is on our side. When the enemy appeared in
sight we had not three bushels of corn. We have since found
in deserted houses 80 or 90 bushels & got into the walls 20
or 30 head of Beeves.

                                                        Travis

I hurried back to my room and within minutes I had written the
Texas education version of Travis's sacred letter:

The (New) Alamo Letter

To: Senator Estes, Representative Hardcastle, Representative
Keffer, and Representative King during these grave times:

Gentlemen,
    I am besieged, by a hundred or more of the Legislators
under Rick Perry. I have sustained a continual Bombardment
of increased high-stakes testing and accountability-related
bureaucracy and a cannonade of gross underfunding for 10
years at least and have lost several good men and women.
The ruling party has demanded another round of pay cuts
and furloughs, while the school house be put to the sword
and our children's lunch money be taken in order to keep
taxes low for big business. I am answering the demand with
a (figurative) cannon shot, and the Texas flag still waves
proudly from our flag pole. I shall never surrender the fight
for the children of Perrin.

> Then, I call on you my legislators in the name of Liberty, of patriotism & everything dear to the American character, to come to our aid, with all dispatch. The enemy of public schools is declaring that spending on a shiny new high-stakes testing system is "non-negotiable"; that, in essence, we must save the test but not the teachers. The enemy of public schools is saying that Texas lawmakers won't raise 1 penny in taxes in order to save our schools.
>
> If this call is neglected, I am determined to sustain myself as long as possible and fight for the kids in these classrooms like an educator who never forgets what is due to his own honor & that of his community. Make education a priority!
>
> With all due respect and urgency,
>
> John Kuhn

I studied the letter for a minute, debated its fate a bit, and then I recklessly emailed it to my hometown newspaper and to Diane Ravitch, the famed author of *The Death and Life of the Great American School System.* As far as I could tell, she was the only person with any kind of clout who was on the side of struggling public schoolteachers. Dr. Ravitch replied and suggested I submit it to a blogger at the *Washington Post* named Valerie Strauss. The next day, the letter appeared online. I got a call from a newspaper reporter from Dallas on my drive home from Austin that afternoon.

That's how I found myself in the middle of this mess. I took sides. I took the side of those who say, "Maybe it isn't all the teachers' fault." Maybe proclaiming schoolteachers as failures when things don't work does little more than to let everyone else—especially politicians—shirk their social obligations to poor children. Maybe it glibly allows political leaders to run away from our biggest challenges and flee our deepest hurts. Maybe this new "reform" narrative stunts the development of real, meaningful reforms both inside and outside the schoolhouse, reforms that will actually improve children's lives. How else do you explain mean-spirited reforms that boosters claim are altruistic toward poor children but that come packaged with an unchallenged inequity of resourcing? In Texas, education reformers love poor children enough to dog their teachers but not enough to fund their schools at anything approaching a level of fairness.

I have many years to go before I can retire. It won't surprise me much if something happens between now and then to make me realize I should've kept my mouth shut and should have, as we tell the kids at the end of their standardized tests, put my pencil down. In the meantime, the reaction to my letter was overwhelmingly positive and inspiring. Teachers, administrators, school lawyers, and parents sent me many dozens of encouraging correspondences.

From there I gave some speeches, including one before 13,000 teachers at a Save Texas Schools rally in Austin and another one a slot or two before Matt Damon spoke at the Save Our Schools March and National Call to Action in Washington, DC. I wrote a number of commentaries and guest blog posts. I encouraged accountability for politicians and, as one writer put it, "radical empathy" for educators. I argued that if competition and labeling really reduce gaps, then our federal government should be consistent and also pursue "data-driven equality"; it should rank and reward the states that most effectively shrink gaps in education-compromising social conditions of their subpopulations.

I demanded more accountability, not less, by calling for desperately needed accountability for the environments in which our teachers teach and our students learn. I said if you're going to fund my school at 85% of the average funding level in the state, then the passing test score for accountability purposes at my school needs to be 85% of the typical passing score.

The 2011 Save Texas Schools Speech

PUBLIC SCHOOL TEACHERS, can you hear me? The school reformers say you are bad at what you do. But the secret to their success is simple: Keep the bad kids out. Exclude the children who are hardest to teach and let them go to public school.

But we say, "Send them to us. We will take them." We say, "Send us your poor; send us your homeless, the children of your afflicted and your addicted. Send us your kids who don't speak English *y nosotros le* [sic] *hablamos en español.* Send us your special needs children; we will not turn them away."

And I tell you today, public school teacher, you will fail to take the shattered children of poverty and turn them into the polished products of the private schools. No, the most damaged public school children will not turn out as shiny and nice and new as the children whose applications are vetted and approved, whose parents buy them books. Nor will you scrub them as clean as those whose parents keep them bundled in the snug blanket of home schooling.

You will be Unacceptable, public school teacher, and I say that is your badge of honor.

I stand before you today bearing proudly the label of "Unacceptable" because I educate the children they will not educate. I, day after day, take these children broken by the policies adopted by the people in this building, and I glue their pieces back together. And at the end of my life you can say those children were better for passing through my sphere of influence.

I am Unacceptable and proud of it.

So I say to this legislature, go ahead and label me. I will march headlong into the teeth of your horrific blame machine, and I will teach these kids.

Millionaire senators, cut my pay back to minimum wage, and still I will march into that classroom full of children who need me. Still I will walk proudly into that classroom with its broken ceiling tiles and burned-out fluorescent bulbs. I will walk forward. Bail out the bankers and bankrupt the teachers. We will still teach!

Bumped and bruised and labeled we will educate these kids because contrary to what they say, I'm not in it for the money. I'm not in it for the benefits. I'm in it because it's right. I'm in it because the children of Perrin, Texas, need somebody like me in their lives.

I'm in it for a 6-year-old little boy right over there named Evan. And for a 9-year-old little boy out there named Noah, and for a

3-year-old little girl named Liliana somewhere in this crowd. I'm in it
for them, and I will fight to secure their future.

I will never follow the lead of those who exclude the ones who
need education the most so that my precious scores will rise.

I will never line up with those whose idea of reform is a subtle
segregation of the poor and desperate.

I want no part of the American caste system.

Look around you. Public school teachers, you are the saviors
of our society and always have been. You are the first responders
standing in this rubble while they sit in their offices and write
judgmental things about you on their clipboards. You are our heroes,
and $27 billion is not near enough for what you're worth. You are
priceless, public schoolteachers of Texas.

So do not be surprised when the men and the women in this
building behind me fail to stand up for you, when they fail to
stand up for the children you serve every day. Their congressional
districts may be rife with poverty, rife with drug abuse, rife with poor
health care, rife with crime, but they will not take on the label of
"Legislatively Unacceptable."

For they do not share the courage of a common schoolteacher.

They do not embrace our accountability. They will not lend
their shoulder to one corner of this sacred burden we bear every
day. They will not sully their hands or let their children play in the
sandbox with the poor. But fear not, for this is our eternal glory. It is
ours to educate. It is theirs to fund or to not fund.

Where our heart is, there will our treasure be also. Let history
judge.

✪ TWO ✪

Scaring America

I THOUGHT MIKE JONES[1] was going to throw a punch at me. This was the same student who had redirected the office computer—the one used by guests to sign in when they visited—to a website promoting the many benefits of smoking weed. If only all his hijinks had been as harmless. One day I got a call that he was on a corner where grown men sold drugs when he was supposed to be in school. I called his mom. She didn't know what to do with him. She'd lost the handle.

Mike wasn't a bad person, but he was a mess of rage. His office referrals were for blatant disrespect, profanity, and threats and aggressively hurtful comments directed at teachers and peers. Whatever was going on inside of him—whether it was chemically induced or just his own hurts bubbling over to this day I don't know—made a successful traditional education incredibly unlikely and brutally hard on both him and his teachers.

Mike had just been in a fight. I knew this because a teacher had walked up on the fight in a stairwell and had collared the other pugilist and brought him to my office. I was an assistant principal then. The victim said Mike was the assailant. (Anytime there's a fight in a high school, each party assures you that he—or, God forbid, *she*—is the victim.)

The teacher and another assistant principal stayed with that kid—himself no angel, mind you—and I went hunting for Mike. A voice in my walkie-talkie said he was scheduled into auto tech that period, so I headed down W-hall where the career and tech teachers lived.

I heard gruff voices as I passed by the W-hall restroom. He was cleaning up the blood.

Mike was at the sink; a lanky kid with patchy scruff on his cheeks stood next to him. I assumed he was getting the blow-by-blow.

"Come on, Mike," I interrupted.

Mike looked up. His face was puffy, with pink streaks and splotches around his eyes.

"Where?" he asked.

"We're going to the office."

"Why?" He got blustery. He always got blustery.

"You were just in a fight."

The lanky kid got out while he could.

"No I wasn't." Mike glared at me through watery eyes from the sink.

"Come on." I turned and walked out the door.

"I'm not going," he declared, but he followed. "I didn't do anything."

"It's on tape, Mike," I argued. I shouldn't have argued. He stopped walking.

"Let's go," I said.

"This is bullshit." He paced back and forth in the hall. I noticed how empty it was. The fluorescent lights hummed.

"Let's go," I said. "We'll talk about it in the office."

I walked and he followed slowly, muttering the whole way.

He paused a few times, but we haltingly made it to the cafeteria before he really dug in.

"I ain't going," he said, pausing to gather the anger. He looked me in the eye. "Bitch."

"You're going, Mike."

The word had felt good. He said it again.

"You're a bitch."

Whatever. Wasn't the first time.

"Let's go."

"Fuck you."

He closed the gap between us. He was clenching and unclenching his fists. The wheels were turning behind his watery eyes. I assumed in his mind he was seeing his fist land against my face. He was seeing me stagger backward, crashing into the windows looking into the big gym, groaning. I was a punk, he was thinking, but in more colorful language. A bookworm and a little punk. He clenched and unclenched both fists.

Maybe it was a show, but it didn't feel like it to me. He was weighing his options. He wanted to do it. What would the other kids think? He'd be a legend. What was the worst that would happen? He'd get in trouble. Big deal, though; he was already in trouble. Get kicked out of school? Probably. It'd be worth it. He never liked me. Nobody liked me. I was a bitch. I had been a bitch since he got to that school. He didn't want to come to this school anyway—this school sucked. Let us kick him out.

Clench. Unclench. I can close my eyes today and still see his. They were bloodshot. They were always bloodshot. I wondered if he was high. Or maybe people just get this mad. My only offense was telling him to go somewhere he didn't want to go. Maybe that was enough to merit a beating.

Clench.

I didn't give him time to make up his mind. I pulled out the radio. "I need Kevin in the cafeteria ASAP," I said.

I made Mike's decision for him. It wasn't just him and me now. Kevin the security man was coming. Kevin was beefy but unarmed; his greatest weapon was the fact that all the kids liked him. It was easy for Mike to hate me, to fantasize about beating me down—I had punished him how many times? But Kevin? Nah, Kevin was cool.

Mike walked on down to the office with Kevin and me in tow, and I climbed into his earhole as soon as he sat down. I let him know just who was in charge around here and just how much trouble he was in. I would've gone easier on him except for one thing: He had scared me.

Spectral Evidence: Scaring Ourselves Into Action

A casual observer of American history might conclude that our nation's finest moments have come in the aftermath of great crises. The Japanese surprise attack on Pearl Harbor, for example, prompted the American leadership to end its policy of restraint and enter fully into World War II against the horrors of the Nazi war machine. This costly decision has been heralded as one of our nation's finest. Tom Brokaw famously dubbed the American men and women of that era our "greatest generation" (Brokaw, 1998).

The same casual observer might also conclude that, from its beginnings, when America has been preemptive, it has more often than not been preemptively bad. If our finest moments have come in responding to real, concrete catastrophes, our worst moments may have been when we responded to extrapolated dangers and supposed risks.

Potential dangers are also potential non-dangers, after all, but don't tell that to our leaders. American politicians and pundits of all stripes cling to imagined and exaggerated fears and dream of utilizing the power of the state to alleviate them; they work overtime convincing the rest of us that their ideological phantasms are real flesh-and-blood monsters that call for concrete action. When the people fall for their scare tactics, bad things tend to happen.

Many panics have seized the American continent. The most notorious was the first.

In the 1600s, Cotton Mather had written a book in which he argued that witches lived among the colonists and performed "astonishing Witchcrafts" (Mather, 1689). Mather's book was exceedingly popular and contained florid descriptions of children in the throes of demonic oppression. According to a contemporary critic, Mather provided "the kindling of those flames, that . . . threatened the destruction of this country" (Calef, n.d., p. 299).

The flames the critic referred to were a figurative wildfire of accusations, trials, and horrifying punishments for witchcraft. There were also literal flames that consumed the bodies of those found guilty in Salem.

Their only "proof" that anyone on trial for witchcraft had supernatural abilities came in the form of the accusers' testimonies and some victims' coerced confessions.

In the absence of real evidence, Cotton Mather himself was instrumental in arguing for the inclusion of something he called "spectral evidence" in the Salem trials. Spectral evidence was merely non-evidence under another name. It was testimony by the accusers that the alleged witches had appeared in a different shape and had tormented them, even though the physical body of the accused might have been present in another place. In this way, spectral evidence had the potential to outweigh actual physical evidence.

Spectral evidence was ultimately permitted in the trials in Salem but not in any other municipality, and a number of citizens were condemned to die in that township because of it.

There is money to be made and political leverage to be exercised if you are willing to scare America. Americans would rather be misled than afraid.

MIKE JONES 2: A MAN AT RISK

I WAS AFRAID WHEN THAT 16-year-old with a thick neck and bloodshot eyes stood inches away from me in an empty cafeteria.

I'm ashamed of the rest of this story, but I'll tell it anyway. Like everyone else, I'm the good guy in most of my memories; but in this one, it isn't so clear-cut. I started out as the good guy. In the hallway with my measured words and my slow, careful movements, and with his unjustified hatefulness, unhinged profanity, and welts on his knuckles from mutual combat between classes, there's no doubt who was the bad guy.

But when we got to my office and closed the door, when I was safe among a blur of other administrators, Kevin the security chief, and the school police officer, I quickly became the villain.

I began to lecture. He protested and I ignored; he raised his voice and I raised mine more. He called me profane names and I kept going. I lectured a kid who didn't need a lecture. He already knew the rules; they just didn't matter to him right then. No matter, I kept going. He punctuated my self-righteous proclamations with one f-bomb after another. Didn't faze me. I kept poking the caged tiger, kept wagging a self-righteous finger in his browbeaten face. He threw every insult he knew at me, and I smiled condescendingly. I was only making things worse, but I didn't care just then.

This would end with him in handcuffs. He would never come back to school; and in those cowardly moments I was absolutely fine with that.

I only cared that he had scared me.

I care now. Wherever he is—not that it does any good—I care. If it's a bad place, it has my fingerprints on it. If it's a good place, it's in spite of me, in spite of that horrible day.

When the campus police officer finally had enough of his threatening and cussing and asked if I wanted him arrested for disturbing the peace, I said yes, absolutely. Get him out of here. My conscience whispered that I was wrong, that I had egged him on. I ignored it. Worse, I walked beside him all the way to the police cruiser door, lecturing him still more. With his hands cuffed behind him, all he could do was tell me over and over again that I was a pussy and a faggot and that I needed to shut the fuck up. But I wouldn't shut up and he couldn't make me, and he cussed just so he didn't have to hear my stupid voice.

I can still hear my stupid voice.

When I turned around and walked back into the building, surreally, my sister was standing there. She was out of place. She was a teacher, but not at that school. Her son was a student, but in a different district. They lived in another town. As far as I knew, she had never been in my building, and yet there she was on my worst day, leaning against the brick wall just inside the front doors, looking at me with a strange expression on her face. Of all days, she had come on this one, on the day of one of the greatest cataclysms I had known in education. She was there because we were hosting a one-act play contest for smaller schools; she had heard and seen it all.

"Is it like that here every day?" she asked.

"You just saw the worst cussing I've ever taken," I replied.

Left unsaid: I deserved every word of it.

As I stood toe to toe with Mike in the cafeteria, the thought of a brawl didn't bother me as much as the thought of monsters lurking on the other side of the battle. What if he knocked me out? What if I knocked him out? What if everyone—my wife, even—lost respect for me? A million horrible potentialities frightened me into action.

I wronged him. He deserved punishment; I owed him a professional service of administering appropriate consequences per our student code of conduct, but I didn't owe him a berating. I wronged him because I was *A Man at Risk*.

I punished Mike for fighting and for "disobeying administrative directives," and he certainly merited punishment for his behavior, but the dressing-down I gave him in the office came from somewhere else. It was a bonus castigation that I doled out for his crime of scaring me with the invisible monsters in my own head.

Mike's punishment should have been a consequence of his misbehavior, not a consequence of my fear. In a perfect world, that brash young assistant principal would recognize in those moments that emotion was in charge and would hand the young man off to a colleague for the dispassionate administration of appropriate consequences. That brash young principal would step away and let reason, not passion, prevail.

"Sell It"

In 2003, American officials decided Iraq warranted an invasion. There were vague hints—spectral evidence, you might say—that Saddam Hussein might have drones, chemical and biological agents, centrifuges, and even yellowcake uranium. President George W. Bush asked Secretary of State Colin Powell to ask the United Nations to support military action.

"We've really got to make the case," the president said. "Maybe they'll believe you" (DeYoung, 2006, p. 3).

Colin Powell gave his speech on February 5, 2003. Lawrence Wilkerson, Powell's chief of staff, opined that Powell's job was to "go up there and sell it" (DeYoung, 2006, p. 4).

And sell it he did. National opinion "shifted literally overnight" in the wake of Powell's speech, and most Americans believed an invasion was justified (DeYoung, 2006, p. 5).

A year after Powell's speech, the head of a group searching for Hussein's weapons told the media that he doubted the weapons ever existed. The invasion was real, and so were the deaths on both sides. But the threat had only been a specter.

Mike Jones 3: Sleepless

M Y SON SLEPT IN THE front room of the house, with a window looking out on Travis Drive. My bedroom was in the back.

A specter wouldn't let me sleep. Every time I closed my eyes, my mind conjured it: Mike Jones's arm waving a pistol out of the passenger window of a car, yelling something as he drove past my house in the middle of the night, firing off two shots blindly.

It wasn't reasonable, but I went and scooped up my son and brought him to sleep in my bed.

The Japanese Scare

With FDR's speech to the nation following Pearl Harbor, there was no "selling it." There was no spectral evidence to massage, no ghost stories to tell: There were 2,000 dead Americans and a smoldering fleet of ships.

But President Roosevelt wasn't immune to making bad decisions based on uncertain (and, ultimately, unreal) dangers. In the aftermath of the attack, certain members of the American military began to question the loyalty of Americans of Japanese descent. The head of Roosevelt's Western Command, Lieutenant General John L. DeWitt, said, "I don't want any of them here. They are a dangerous element. . . . [W]e must worry about the Japanese all the time until he is wiped off the map" (Toyosaburo, 1944, footnote 2).

Japanese Americans were alleged to be impossible to assimilate, to be engaged in espionage, and to be irreparably loyal to their homeland during hostilities.

President Roosevelt signed Executive Order 9066 in February 1942, and Japanese internment camps would eventually hold more than 100,000 Japanese Americans ("The truth," 2011).

There is a wealth of documentation demonstrating the hysteria surrounding Japanese internment, including government reports clouded by racial antipathy. But a report from the Office of Naval Intelligence "found that only a small percentage of Japanese Americans posed a potential security threat, and that the most dangerous were already known or in custody" ("The truth," 2011). The existence of this report, known as the Ringo report, was suppressed by the U.S. Solicitor General in trials brought before the Supreme Court by two Japanese Americans who challenged their detentions. Not only did the solicitor obscure the report, but he also failed to "inform the Court that a key set of allegations used to justify the internment, that Japanese Americans were using radio transmitters to communicate with enemy submarines off the West Coast, had been discredited by the FBI and FCC. And to make matters worse, he relied on gross generalizations" (Katyal, 2011).

Both men's detentions were upheld by the Supreme Court. Their convictions wouldn't be overturned until almost 50 years later (Katyal, 2011). Justice would come in 1988, when President Ronald Reagan signed legislation apologizing for the government's role in the debacle, establishing an education fund, and paying reparations to surviving internees (Hatamiya, 1999, p. 190).

There was real evidence in existence all along that Japanese Americans did not merit internment. The state not only concealed that exculpatory evidence, but it also manufactured accusatory evidence out of nothing, stitching together wisps of hearsay from the ether into a hazy monster scary enough to let them win their case.

Spectral evidence can get things done, but it has a poor track record of leading us in the right direction. When the U.S. government joins Chicken Little's chorus, it doesn't mean the sky is actually falling.

Birth of a Meme

Official government reports regarding the nature and quality of the American education system date back to at least 1947, with the Higher Education for American Democracy report to U.S. President Harry S. Truman. Other education reports followed.

Of all the reports, 1983's *A Nation at Risk* is the most well-known, and has had the greatest impact on education policy, practice, and national attitudes toward public education in the United States.

A Nation at Risk has been praised by many since its publication, but it has also been derided as a grave misdiagnosis. Greg Toppo, writing for *USA Today* on the 25th anniversary of the report, noted

that "depending on your point of view, [*A Nation at Risk*] either ruined public education or saved it" (Toppo, 2008). One fan of the report said it was the "catalyst of the 'excellence movement' that still
rocks us," while a critic declared it "an overstatement of the problem, and it led to . . . hysterical responses" (Toppo, 2008, sidebar).

The sense of emergency in the document is undeniable. It urges
action, and quickly. "History is not kind to idlers," it declares (National Commission on Excellence in Education, 1983). It goes on to
state that other countries are becoming more economically productive and more competitive than ever before (National Commission
on Excellence in Education, 1983). It lists a handful of indicators of
the risk, including:

- American students weren't first or second on 19 separate
  international tests
- 23 million American adults couldn't read, nor could 13% of
  17-year-olds
- the average performance of American students on the SAT
  had declined from 1963 to 1980
- remedial math classes had increased at the college level by
  72%
- many naval recruits were entering training unable to read
  training manuals, which were written at a 9th-grade level
  (National Commission on Excellence in Education, 1983).

The report was well-received by those who would propagate its
dire message of existential danger and imminent national downfall.
"*A Nation at Risk* played big in the media," noted Gerald Bracey on
the report's 20th birthday. "In the month following its publication,
the *Washington Post* carried 28 stories about it. Few were critical"
(Bracey, 2003, p. 617). Bracey noted too that "universities and education associations fell all over themselves lauding" *A Nation at Risk*, in
part to avoid appearing "defensive" (Bracey, 2003, p. 621).

The warning of *A Nation at Risk* proved to be the first of many.
"Our schools are failing" became a well-worn phrase in educational discourse. Like the anti-Japanese commentary that spread

virulently through American journalism and kitchen table talk after Pearl Harbor, this sweeping stereotype impugning a large number of innocent Americans took root in our collective consciousness and was widely accepted and propagated with little to no critical examination or disagreement. "Our schools are failing" became the expression of a popular, enduring American dogma built upon a foundation of cherry-picked data, and the cherry-picking started in *A Nation at Risk*. Each of the bulleted points above from that report has been forcefully and factually rebutted by thinkers like Gerald Bracey, Richard Rothstein, and Diane Ravitch (and many others), but the fearsome myth persists. Why?

Why do Americans believe their schools are failing? Interestingly, polling data shows that most Americans don't actually believe *their own* public schools are failing; they believe that *all those other American public schools* are failing. Diane Ravitch puts it this way:

> Most Americans graduated from public schools, and most went from school to college or the workplace without thinking that their school had limited their life chances. . . . The annual Gallup poll about education shows that Americans are overwhelmingly dissatisfied with the quality of the nation's schools, but 77 percent of public school parents award their own child's public school a grade of A or B, the highest level of approval since the question was first asked in 1985. (Ravitch, 2011)

How can it be that so many Americans are simultaneously satisfied with the public schools their children attend and dissatisfied with American schools in general? Their opinion of their children's school—based on their experiences with the school itself, its people, its facilities, and its programs—is overwhelmingly positive. But where do they get their negative opinion of all those other schools, the ones that are "out there," that they've never seen but have scary mental pictures of?

With pundits, politicians, journalists, and the murmuring class all repeating the party line that "our schools are failing" since 1983, is it any wonder? When former DC superintendent and perennial school reform superstar Michelle Rhee has her well-funded political group run an advertisement during the Olympics "featuring a disheveled athlete trying and failing to effectively compete," purporting to highlight "the struggles of America's education system and its challenges competing internationally," is it any wonder ("Michelle Rhee appears," 2012)? When famed documentary filmmaker Davis Guggenheim makes a huge splash with an unashamedly propagandistic film that selectively portrays public schools in a harsh light and portrays hand-picked charter schools in pastels, contending that they alone will save America from its disastrous public schools, is it any wonder?

Then there are the accountability systems that have taken hold from coast to coast. Pushed as a way for America to get a good look at its schools, high-stakes testing and its attendant ranking and sorting schemes have devolved into a collection of grotesque funhouse mirrors, designed not to report but to distort the performance of schools and teachers by overemphasizing certain traits and concealing others. Advocates of this kind of accountability, touting something they call "rigor," have designed progressively narrower and harder tests and trumpeted the results—surprise, poor communities do poorly!—in an advertising campaign akin to the television commercials that use magnified pictures of the pores on ladies' noses to scare daytime television viewers into buying sticky strips to pull the dirt out.

The unapologetic rank mendacity started with that 1983 report. For all its talk of a rising tide of mediocrity, *A Nation at Risk* spurred a "rising tide of negative reports," and a "cottage industry of national reports by people saying how bad things are," according to one educator (Toppo, 2008). Richard Rothstein generously notes that "*A Nation at Risk* was well-intentioned, but based on flawed analyses, at least some of which should have been known to the commission that authored it. The report burned into Americans' consciousness a conviction that, evidence notwithstanding, our schools are failures" (Rothstein, 2008). *A Nation at Risk* was the groundbreaking inspiration for a generation of liars and saboteurs, reckless mishandlers of evidence who worried first about their agendas and last about the Socratic pursuit of truth.

The most potent fear exploited by the *Risk* authors was the fear of waning American influence. It was a low blow, a craven appeal to the deeply held fear all of us naturally possess for our children's safety. To illustrate this danger, they contended that American students were never first or second on 19 different international tests and were dead last seven times (National Commission on Excellence in Education, 1983). They neglected to mention that, as Diane Ravitch has noted, "our nation has never had high scores on those tests. When the first international test was given in 1964, our students ranked 11th out of 12 nations. Yet our nation went on to become the most powerful economy in the world" (Ravitch, 2012). Furthermore, many of the countries against which American scores were compared gave the tests to select students, while the United States gave it to a representative cross-section of its population. David C. Berliner and Bruce J. Biddle noted in their influential book *The Manufactured Crisis* that "differences [in test-taker selection] mean that American student achievement scores may look bad simply because they are gathered from the full range of students in the country, whereas scores from other countries are gathered from biased samples" (1995, p. 54).

In a 2011 interview, Berliner put it bluntly: "the people who are saying we look terrible in international competition are simply lying" (School Leadership Briefing, 2011).

Fear Sells

In 1956, the first cleaning solution to be marketed in a spray bottle was a spray-on tire and upholstery cleaner marketed by the Spray Nine Corporation. The innovative company had unleashed "an entirely new product category" known as "the ready-to-use, spray-on/wipe-off cleaner" (Illinois Tool Works, 2011).

Spray Nine is still on the market today. It's known as a cleaning agent so effective that NASA uses it (Walton, 2000). The popular cleaning agent found new usefulness in 1968 when a disinfectant was added to the formula and it moved from the garage to the countertop. From there the Spray Nine brand expanded to include a full line of products with a variety of household and professional applications.

Spray Nine's innovations, however, have not been limited to revolutionary packaging and timely formula adjustments. In 1995, a marketing consultant called a Spray Nine labeling change "an advertising breakthrough" ("Marketing," 1995). What dramatic change did the company make to the iconic cleaner's label? They simply added a short note guaranteeing that Spray Nine would kill the virus that causes AIDS in 30 seconds flat. This was in 1995, the same year that Greg Louganis disclosed that he was HIV-positive ("A Timeline," n.d.).

Did the promotional breakthrough work? According to a spokesman for the company, sales grew by at least 25% in the 2 years after the AIDS-related notice was added to the product (Walton, 2000, p. 5). This was despite the fact that the HIV virus is "so fragile that almost anything . . . will cause it to die" (Walton, 2000, p. 5) and that it "will die even if you put nothing on it" ("Marketing," 1995).

Fear sells. Whether the exploitation of fear was the point of the notice is debatable. Spray Nine claimed they were simply marketing to hospitals and nurses. Nonetheless, even if Spray Nine's marketers weren't deliberately playing on the AIDS scare of the early 1990s, the company undoubtedly won new customers who chose their product out of concern—rational or not—about HIV.

What's the harm in using fear to sell a product or a political argument? If a sprinkling of fear can grease the skids, does it really hurt to play fast and loose with a few facts or to exaggerate a danger here or there?

It hurt a lot if you were Japanese American in the early 1940s. Or an American public school student or teacher after 1983.

✪ THREE ✪

Standardized Junk Science

THIS KID—WE'LL CALL HIM JOE—was a solid kid. He wasn't a brain and didn't care to be. He wasn't going to get elected class president or play first trumpet in the band or star in a drama production. He wasn't trying to impress; he was just what he was, and he didn't try to make up for average academics with charm or cheekiness. He just played it cool.

A KID LIKE DENIM

JOE MONTES BARELY SPOKE at all around adults. He wasn't even close to a teacher's pet, but he was anything but a bad kid. He didn't get his kicks by being mean to underclassmen or showing off for the girls. He carried himself more like a man than a boy.

Joe liked sports, and I'd guess girls and cars. But definitely sports. He was good enough to make all-district. Not good enough to get an athletic scholarship, sadly, but plenty good enough to be a quality contributor to the team and to make memories and friendships that he'll never forget.

In any other era in American education, Joe would have graduated without much trouble. His teachers, recognizing who he was in a way that a test just couldn't, would've seen to it that he walked the stage—and he would've gone on to make a good living as a quality contributor in someone's business, maybe his own. He would have likely worked with his hands, quietly and effectively: HVAC installation, maybe? Plumbing? Electrical?

In any other era in American education, Joe wouldn't have been deemed a failure just because the sterile comfort of a college classroom didn't appeal to him.

Some might've called Joe a "jock," but that would be grossly inaccurate. There were more nuances to him than that. He was on the team and he wore his letter jacket, but he was anything but a towel-popper.

I didn't worry about Joe one bit as he worked his way through school. He stayed out of trouble outside of school and he never got sent to the office. His grades weren't stellar, but he passed. He managed to get by even though he was narrowly passing every year on his state testing.

When Joe and his mom came into my office around Christmas his senior year, I was surprised. This was no high-maintenance mom; I'd never met her. She was pretty and sweet and she smiled kindly, but her eyes were puffy from crying.

"What can I do for you?" I asked.

She was embarrassed by the whole situation. She didn't know what to do. Joe stood apart from us, close to the door so he could get this over with and get out as quickly as possible.

"He wants to quit school," she said.

"What?"

I couldn't believe it. There were kids who could've quit school that day and it wouldn't have surprised me, but not this one. Joe was exactly the blue collar kind of kid that high school graduations were made for. He *had to* walk across the stage. A graduation ceremony is the closest thing we have to an American seal of approval for a young person getting ready to spread his or her wings.

In my mind, Joe was a carbon copy of my dad as a teenager: a low-key kid who just wanted to play sports and get out of school and raise a family on the strength of his labor and character. He was the great kind of all-around student who makes the "all successful kids must be prepared for college" myth crumble to pieces. Joe wasn't interested in college. I'm not able to bring myself to say, smugly, that he wasn't "college material." But I don't believe for a second that was what he wanted for himself.

And that matters.

Whether or not he was college material, Joe was great life material. Joe was denim, as opposed to silk, and there are applications in this world for which silk is distinctly unsuited. A nation with a school system that devalues rugged skills is doomed to be a nation that can't fix its broken things.

My dad tried to drop out of school once. He'd had enough. His mom wouldn't sign the papers to let him join the Navy, though, and his agriculture teacher Mr. Henry—of whom my dad speaks reverently still today—convinced him to finish. A high school diploma is something no one can ever take away, he'd told my dad.

Dad did graduate, and he became a firefighter for the city of Dallas. He fought fires for 27 years. They used to say he could chop a hole in a roof faster than anyone, his high school math scores notwithstanding.

But I'm no Mr. Henry.

"Joe?" I asked, looking him in the eye. Joe looked away. He didn't have anything to say. He didn't want any part of whatever I had to say.

"He says he can't pass the math test," his mom said. She was talking about the TAKS, the Texas Assessment of Knowledge and Skills, a set of four tests high school juniors were required to pass in order to graduate. Joe had passed the other three.

"I can't," he finally spat. His eyes were welling. This was the only time I ever saw Joe not be the coolest person in the room. "I've taken it three times."

"Joe, you get another chance before graduation," I told him. He already knew.

"That's what I told him," she said. "He won't listen."

Joe's mom looked at me desperately. *Save my boy.*

"I told him I want him to graduate," she said. Her tears were flowing now. "I told him that's what I want." I handed her the box of tissues I kept in my office.

"You're the mom," I told her. "If you want him in school, he has to stay in school."

She shook her head. It wasn't that simple.

"He says he'll stop coming."

I hadn't thought of that. I hadn't thought of Joe defying his mom and me and the whole system. Normally, he probably wouldn't have done such a thing, not gratuitously. He wasn't like that. But he was finished taking TAKS tests, come what may.

"What will happen if he stops coming to school?" she asked.

I grimaced. "We would file truancy charges. He would go to court and the judge would either give him another chance, or else give him a fine." I didn't know what else to tell her. The only other option was to say that we wouldn't press charges—that we wouldn't criminalize this stellar kid and would simply nag him and pester him to give up any real leverage to get him to attend.

"We can't afford a fine," she said.

"I'm not coming," Joe said softly, but adamantly. Mom wasn't big enough to make him. Neither was I. Joe had *de facto* school choice, and he was exercising it.

"He wants me to withdraw him to home school," she said. Home school—the savvy Texas teen's ever-present trump card.

Maybe Mom wanted me to save her from the inevitability of the decision she knew she would make. Or maybe she just hoped beyond hope that I could talk some sense into Joe.

I couldn't.

JOE MONTES 2: JOE AND THE PACKET LADY

SHE AND I BOTH KNEW the type of home school Joe was asking for wasn't the legitimate kind in which a considerate parent seeks out valid educational materials or a home school cooperative and ensures that their child learns something. It was, instead, a feel-good non-education that dozens of other local students had cheerily signed up for over the years.

The home school he was asking for was merely a get-out-of-school-free card provided by a local woman known by some as the Packet Lady. Her unaccredited "private school" allowed students to earn a diploma in a matter of weeks or months.

She reportedly charged $100 per month, per student for her services as a home school consultant, and the kids only had to take classes—that is, fill out (or have a friend or parent fill out) packets of photocopied worksheets—for the courses in which they lacked credits on their high school transcripts. No TAKS tests were required. Plus, the Packet Lady's scholars reported to me that they got a break on tuition for each student they recruited from surrounding schools.

These kids sometimes came back for sporting events. "I finished high school!" they would say, often a few short months after they had left. I always feigned enthusiasm for their watered-down credential, but inside I died. What they had gotten was a piece of paper, not an education.

I cajoled Joe. He wasn't the kind of kid you could cajole too much, but I gave him a pretty good spiel about the importance of education, about how he had been with his class for so long and how he really ought to graduate with them. I told him he should stick around to see how he would do on the next retake. I assured him that a real diploma was worth more to employers than something from a diploma mill. I told him no one could ever take away a diploma once he earned it.

He said that was true of the easy-breezy home school diploma, too.

It was no use. Joe's mom thanked me, and then she walked with her son to my secretary's office and wrote a letter saying she wanted to home-school him. We had no recourse but to accept the letter and withdraw the student. The teenager had won, and lost.

I don't know that I've ever felt more defeated watching a kid walk out the door. My dad only got a diploma because a man did what I was unable to do that day. Despite my best efforts, a solid kid walked away from school, convinced he was a failure.

Joe should have graduated. Who gets the blame that he didn't? Was it his math teachers, going all the way back to elementary, who never got through to him with math facts in a way that mattered, who never convinced him that math was worth learning? Or did the blame belong to Joe himself, who perhaps never applied himself in the classroom the way he should've? Or should we blame the test, an instrument of mere measurement, a messenger telling how much or how little a child knows about a given subject? Or should we blame the stakes attached to the test, arbitrary punishments set by distant overlords and applied blindly—in a standardized fashion— with no flex for cases like Joe, good kids—great kids—successful kids with one single blemish on their high school career that just so happens through the caprices of political fates to be the one detail, the one subject, that can cost them their caps and gowns and their pomp and their circumstance?

There is enough blame to go around, I guess. Some of Joe's teachers may have phoned it in. And Joe probably goofed off too much once he lost the handle on math. And I get my lumps too. Maybe my supervision was inadequate in his high school classrooms. But we must not exempt the system from criticism while we bash the teachers and the student for their failures. A true accounting of kids like Joe would necessarily add more than math and ELA test scores to the ledger of his human success; a system that fails to do this is as flawed as the worst of the bad teachers.

"Applying Objective Measures Badly"

Today we've traded voodoo for jargon and magic for something approaching science. We don't believe in witches and bogeymen, but we can't walk away from our subtler irrationalities; we aren't yet brave enough to bury our totems. As a result, we dress up things that aren't really facts in mendacious semi-logic and pretend we are converting our beliefs, hopes, and desires—non-facts all—into inviolable and inarguable truths.

When science doesn't give us what we want, we turn to pseudoscience.

Though it is rolling at a full boil today, the American love affair with standardized tests began tepidly. In World War I, Army Mental Tests were used to sort servicemen into various roles (Fletcher, 2009). The first bubble tests arrived in the 1930s, and today tests like the SAT, ACT, and GED are ubiquitous (Fletcher, 2009). If a little testing is good, a lot of testing must be better. And if testing is good for finding out what students know, then it follows that it must be equally good for finding out how well teachers teach.

Gradually, policymakers learned to dismiss the advice of testing professionals who insisted their tests be used for prescribed applications—for example, a test of student knowledge is precisely that. It isn't a test of teaching quality. But this is very inconvenient. Lawmakers have objective data about student learning, and they want objective data about teacher quality. Using a tool designed to measure student learning in order to gauge teachers' instructional quality doesn't seem like a bridge too far.

As the off-label application of student testing data has become prevalent, a great fissure has opened up between two camps of education professionals. Everyone essentially agrees that teachers receive students into their classrooms with vastly different readiness levels. Judging teachers based on whether all of their students achieve an absolute minimum score is universally recognized as unfair. But some policy professionals believe fervently in a new breed of "value-added" algorithm that they claim is able to take the data and correct for both differences in students' prior knowledge and outside influences the teacher can't control, thereby allowing the students' work to reveal who is a good or a bad teacher. These measures don't look at absolute scores but rather improvement in each student's score during the year spent with the teacher. The real magic—and faith—comes in when the algorithm attempts to set a predicted amount of improvement that each student *ought to have made*; the teacher is rated based on how often he or she outperforms the individual improvement called for by the algorithm.

The other camp vigorously opposes this brave new world of prediction-reliant appraisal. These are people who feel that student test results are affected by too many other factors to give a clear picture of one teacher's instructional quality.

The people with the more cautious and nuanced view of the situation are mostly teachers and their representatives: that is, the people whose livelihoods are directly affected by the implementation of these new techniques. Failure of these systems to work as advertised for them could be personally catastrophic. Meanwhile, those most blithe about rolling out the value-added measures are typically a little farther away from the classroom; say, in a think tank somewhere.

Everyone is listening to the sound from these tests. Half the audience claims they have a magic tool that lets them hear music; the other half says it's still mostly noise.

In an epoch of austere budgets, the state cannot afford to subsidize bad teaching. Lawmakers hope beyond hope that value-added works. They *need* it to work. Therein is the root of their dogged faith.

Standardized testing has gone from tool to tenet. At one time, standardized tests in schools were used explicitly according to instructions. In recent years, however, no less of an authority than the federal government has called for extending student test results beyond their prescribed meaning.

Others have carried this unproven new method out to yet another degree. They want to use student scores to rate the educator preparation programs that produce the educators who teach the children who take the tests. This is akin to castigating the maiden who milked the cow that tossed the dog that worried the cat that killed the rat that ate the malt if there happens to be a problem with the house that Jack built. Soon they'll ask to use 4th-graders' math scores to rate the institutions that granted the graduate degrees to the professors who teach in the educator preparation programs. It's the Six Degrees of Standardized Testing game, and there seems to be no end to the extension of testing.

Makers of the tests will tell you they're not made to do these things, but the advocates assure everyone that they can pull it off with absolute accuracy and validity. The new algorithms can alleviate the concerns of the psychometricians and, they are certain, accomplish the amazing and longed-for feat of accurate and objective appraisal twice-removed.

Teachers aren't so sure, and the science is painfully suspect. Value-added measures have been rushed into use with no independent verification that they work as promised, with potentially devastating results for the nation's schools.

We all pursue airbrushed information and cherry-picked statistics that will uphold our precious orthodoxies. It is human nature. We desperately defend our self-lies from intruding reality by constructing elaborate systems to almost-prove they're true. This is what is being done in defense of value-added measures of teacher quality. Nothing proves they work, but nothing needs to. There is faith parading as science at work here.

The intrusion of actual science into comfortable pretend-science worlds was beautifully illustrated when Nate Silver started his presidential-race handicapping tool at www.fivethirtyeight.com. A wunderkind sabermetrician, Silver developed a highly successful program to forecast baseball players' performance before turning his attention—and his prowess for interpreting data—to the 2008 presidential election. He started the aforementioned blog and on it rightly predicted the popular presidential vote in 49 out of 50 states, along with every single race contested for the U.S. Senate that year.

Pundits took great offense during the 2012 election as Silver's tool—nothing more than an average of polls, really, with each one painstakingly weighted to correct for bias—contradicted their own shamanistic proclamations. They stood nakedly revealed as charlatans, and they didn't like it. One of them, Joe Scarborough, publicly derided Silver for contending that the race between Mitt Romney and Barack Obama wasn't a dead heat and mocked him for having the audacity to pretend his statistical analysis could predict the outcome (Scarborough, 2012). The conflict between Silver and Scarborough was a collision of pure, thoroughly vetted science and the quick and dirty junk science of cherry-picking punditry. Scarborough issued a half-hearted apology after Silver nailed the outcome in 50 out of 50 states (Daley, 2012).

I understand the irony of calling on a good algorithm to refute the implementation of bad algorithms, but opposition to value-added measures among educators isn't based on some backward rejection of scientific advancements. Algorithms aren't the bad guy; reckless algorithms are. Tests aren't the bad guy; the misuse of testing is.

Value-added algorithms as we currently know them simply lack the care in construction and implementation that Silver practiced in building his tool, and Silver's tool mostly only impacts gamblers. If we are going to fire public servants based on algorithms, they must be at least as perfect as Nate Silver's. They aren't, but some nevertheless choose to pretend they are reliable enough to determine whose reputations, careers, and futures go up in smoke. Nate Silver himself—the so-called "Lord and God of the Algorithm"—has expressed his doubts (Dwyer, 2013).

"There are certainly cases where applying objective measures badly is worse than not applying them at all, and education may well be one of those," said Silver in a Reddit "Ask Me Anything" event, when asked specifically about using student test scores to judge teacher quality (Dwyer, 2013).

One researcher—Stanford University's Edward Haertel—discouraged the high-stakes use of value-added measures due to the fact that they could be "systematically biased *for* some teachers and *against* others" (Haertel, 2013, pp. 23–24, emphasis in original in all quotes), and that "sorting teachers according to single-year value-added scores is sorting mostly on noise" (p. 18). Haertel noted that value-added measures will not "simply reward or penalize teachers according to how well or poorly they teach. They will *also* reward or penalize teachers according to *which students* they teach and *which schools* they teach in" (p. 13) and "should emphatically *not* be included as a substantial factor . . . in consequential teacher personnel decisions" (p. 23).

The Fragile Linchpin

Not only value-added measuring systems but also school accountability systems are somewhat like the dowsing rods of education. Via inscrutable scientific mechanics or some unexplained magnetism, they alert us when they tease out great teaching from among cells of student test data.

Because these school- and teacher-ranking systems are built on mathematics, they are presented as unassailably objective. They aren't. The tests themselves may be objective—I'll leave conversations about test validity to the experts—but the structures elaborated on the tests are often fraught with subjectivity and perfectly suited for behind-the-scenes manipulation.

No matter how easy or hard a test may be, passing rates can be set as high or as low as the state desires. Want to say schools are doing great? Just make the questions easier or reduce the number of correct answers needed to pass. In 2009, during the heady days of the so-called "New York Miracle," state officials fell all over themselves in self-congratulation as 82% of students passed their math exams and 69% passed their English exams (Gentilviso, 2010). One year later, after the state revamped the tests, scores plummeted to 54% and 42%, respectively, leaving officials to explain why scores had risen and fallen so abruptly.

Scores had risen because the tests were watered down in 2006, and post-dilution, officials didn't hesitate to declare miraculous education results under their amazing leadership, attributing the rising scores not to an easing up on the tests but rather to their own skillful implementation of policy.

In New York, John Dewey had left the building, and he was replaced by a band of merry salesmen. In the aftermath of the collapse of New York state's test scores, the *New York Times* noted that the "fast rise and even faster fall" of test scores "involved direct warnings that went unheeded" and an "administration that trumpeted gains in student performance despite its own reservations about how reliably the test gauged future student success" (Medina, 2010). A former city testing chief noted that schools "were duped into thinking they were making these incredible gains . . . when in reality they were not" (Monahan, Lesser, & Kolodner, 2010).

Despite the shenanigans, the faith of the mayor of New York City in the almost-science of school reform held firm. "This mayor uses

data and metrics to determine whether policies are failing or succeeding," said one surrogate (Medina, 2010). The surrogate failed
to mention if the mayor cared whether the metrics he used were
reliable.

Student testing, it turns out, is a fragile linchpin on which to hang
our nation's future. Being data-driven is good enough; being *valid
data*-informed is scorned as overly cautious or insufficiently radical.

Scary times, of course, call for radical actions.

The genius of Nate Silver—and it's sad that this qualifies for genius, really—is that he was unsatisfied with crappy data. If only anyone in the school data game were as picky. Silver looked for the signal
in the noise, to paraphrase the title of his best-selling book, and he
found it fairly simply: by averaging polls together and then providing probabilities in place of proclamations. While pundits delivered
a constant stream of gut-feeling analysis, armchair prognostication,
and relentless gaffe-spotting, and while traditional polling organizations used comfortable but reckless methodologies (like conducting
polls only over landlines), Silver stuck with his honest and thorough
science, and he held fast to no sacred totems (Lamare, 2012).

In the end, the polling firms that Silver embarrassed were, like
today's education reformers, unwilling to "let the perfect be the enemy of the good." More precisely, they were unwilling to let the accurate be the enemy of the facile.

As if to prove that we cling to our old idols even in the face of
strong evidence of their impotence, after Nate Silver nailed the election and the long-prominent Gallup called it for Romney, Americans
said they trusted Gallup over Silver by a margin of 31 to 14% (Halperin, 2012). Who cares that this is the same company that called the
Truman election for Dewey? We feel good about them, we've heard
of them, and we aren't really all that interested in getting to the truth.
We will settle for comfortable approximations.

Meanwhile, the stakes tied to our school accountability sciences
should be far too high for us to be content with shoddy data; these
stakes have names like Joe.

The Façade Cracks

Robert Scott was the Commissioner of Education in Texas as test-based accountability grew more and more central and controlling. Near the end of his term, he surprised many when he responded to a question from the State Board of Education by saying an overemphasis on testing had become a "perversion" (Weiss, 2012). A short time later, he gave a speech to an annual gathering of superintendents that left us all agape.

Before Scott began, I asked a superintendent friend sitting next to me what he expected to hear and he grumbled, "If it's like last year, it won't be anything good."

Scott surprised all of us. He launched into a critique of the limitations and abuses of testing and accountability that none of us had heard outside of our faculty meetings and superintendent gatherings. He said testing had gotten out of hand and he looked forward to rolling it back. We clapped like we had never clapped before at a superintendents' conference.

After Texas education commissioner Robert Scott became a heretic by daring to publicly call into question the widely accepted inerrancy of test-based accountability, the ire of dogmatists was aroused. Senator Florence Shapiro said she was "blown away" by Scott's comments. "He's been the one that's been talking about school accountability over the years. We've all been a part of this. School accountability is something we started many, many years ago, and we believe in it," she said (Smith, 2012b).

Meanwhile, Bill Hammond, the head of the Texas Association of Business and Texas's most vocal testing cheerleader, accused Scott of "making excuses for the educators" (Smith, 2012b). Just as the shamans bashed Nate Silver for the honesty inherent in his use of probabilities, the accountability brigade couldn't abide Scott's critical take on testing and his politically inexpedient honesty about the limitations of accountability.

A Promising Bud

A LEX[1] SAT ACROSS THE TABLE from me. His dad sat beside him in a 60s-style leather biker cap, with an abiding scowl and wispy black facial hair. We were there to talk about Alex's testing and his future. He was a senior.

Alex was a star in Mr. Hardin's metal shop. Mr. Hardin was in the meeting, ready, willing, and able to brag on his prized pupil. Alex had taken all the metal classes we offered, going all the way back to his freshman year, and he had shown an aptitude for a variety of discrete metalworking tasks.

But Alex's greatest strength was his creativity and artistry with a welder. He'd aced the high school art class he took, but his inner Rembrandt didn't fully come out on sketch paper or in trash art projects. His muse sang loudest in the shop, where the acrid smell of burnt wire hung in the air. His greatest masterpiece, in fact, was proudly displayed in one corner of Mr. Hardin's immaculately ordered welding shop.

Alex came by his skill honestly. His dad had worked with his hands his whole life.

Our conversation around the table quickly revealed Alex's dad to be a hard man, a no-holds-barred kind of guy who wanted nothing but the best for his son. He was the scowling sort who would defend you to the death if you treated him and his kid right, but he would also tell you just what he thought of you if you didn't, and not necessarily in school-appropriate terms.

We praised Alex thoroughly, only partially out of fear of his old man. For the most part, our accolades were the product of that extremely common teacher trait of wanting to encourage the promising buds we catch peeking out of the garden so that we might feel good about our own green thumbs when they flourish. Encouraging the most promising kids helps us convince ourselves that we're benefiting society with our lives; it gives us the endurance to get out of bed in the mornings and carry on.

Alex had lots of promise. His grades were good. He'd met his graduation requirements, except for one: like Joe, Alex had failed the exit-level TAKS math test three times.

Along with dozens of our students, Alex annually competed in an interscholastic vocational contest to show off what he was learning. He had reached the pinnacle of success with his metal project that year, scoring high at the regional contest and representing our school at the state level.

Teams and individuals from across the state entered their projects. I don't remember what place Alex took, but I remember his teacher beaming in the office when they got back, telling us all how proud he was of his welding Da Vinci as he placed a trophy on our front counter for display.

Alex had made a smoker, that most Texan of trailer-mounted contraptions. It was big enough to feed a football team. It had all the bells and whistles, including an actual dinner bell. It had a temperature gauge and handmade slots for spatulas and tongs. It had cup holders; we teachers agreed they were meant to hold Dr Peppers and not other beverages. Alex had welded his name and the year into the thing, and he had adorned it with a variety of Texas stars and stylized longhorn heads. The project was proof of his extraordinary technical proficiency, an amazing aptitude that portended great success for Alex after high school.

The state disagreed with our silly hopefulness regarding Alex's future, however. Alex was too awful at math to be loosed upon the world with a diploma. There was no TAKS test for welding or art for Alex to show the state how and where he shone, and Alex was not very interested in learning the math the state wanted to see. Alex had a little bit of his dad in him: He wouldn't easily conform to the world or the Texas Education Agency.

So Alex, being a stubborn individualist and a fairly indifferent mathematician, was doomed to dropping out, except for one saving grace: He had a diagnosed learning disability. Based on that, Alex was allowed to demonstrate mastery of math via his Individual Education Plan, without having to pass the math TAKS test. Unlike Joe, he would graduate.

We explained all this to Alex and his dad, but it struck me then that it was all nothing but noise to them. I think the only words they really heard were, "Alex will graduate." To Alex and his dad, everything else—the testing, the meetings, the forms and signatures, and all the smiling teachers—it was all fundamentally irrelevant when compared to the thought of his son walking across that stage.

The God Number

Robert Scott wasn't finished. After resigning his post and accepting a job with an Austin law firm, Scott spoke freely about what testing and accountability had become in an interview with the *Dallas Morning News*. He called for a "midcourse correction" to the Texas accountability system in an interview that echoed concerns long-raised by Lone Star teachers and superintendents (Weiss, 2012). In the interview, Scott addressed the withering criticism he had taken from people like Pearson lobbyist Sandy Kress, who had accused Scott of "retail demagoguing" (Smith, 2012b). Scott responded by saying his comments weren't part of a "grand plan" to start an anti-testing revolution (Smith, 2012b). Then he acknowledged something that a Pearson lobbyist would never freely admit: The heart of the entire accountability regime was a single, arbitrarily chosen number. Noting the crux of what makes testing in no way an objective measure of academic achievement, Scott said, "I'm the guy who set the passing standard for five years" (Smith, 2012b).

Each year, one man single-handedly selected a number that determined whether 100 schools were failures, or whether 10 were. This was what was behind the curtain; this was the supposed science of school accountability.

"When you use [standardized testing] for so many high-stakes things, and you know it's fallible, you know there are risks," Scott said (Smith, 2012b).

Texas's vaunted accountability system for schools enabled a political appointee to simply pull a number out of the air and call it passing, driving via that single arbitrary act an entire state's perception of the quality of its public schools and the people who staffed them. This entire enterprise was ripe for mischief, and Scott admitted it.

Contrary to what the public was led to believe by boosters for test-driven reform, neither the test nor the rankings derived from them were ever an objective measure of academic achievement. It was all political theater. Their dire warnings were bugaboos for the papers, no more real than the imbedded Japanese spies on ham radios that never existed during World War II.

Robert Scott had the singular audacity to point out the clay feet of school accountability, the fatal flaw that goes unacknowledged by eager testing advocates, the foundational weakness in their architecture that screams for attention: The system is purely and foundationally subjective, and that subjectivity has been systematically obscured from parents and journalists from the get-go, airbrushed away with imperious statements about the system's efficacy, squelched with the recurrent disarming allegation that anyone who questions conventional testing wisdom necessarily doesn't care about children.

Test-based accountability from birth was imbued with nothing more than a pretend objectivity; high-stakes decisions were made based on random cut points pulled out of somebody's hat. As newspapers fell all over themselves reporting that Texas schools were in major trouble one year, or making tremendous gains the next, Scott had to live with the inconvenient knowledge that he had a finger on a single switch that could magically create a great hand-wringing over the inexcusable failures of Texans like my sisters and me, or a great celebration of our success. Robert Scott could make me or break me—and thousands like me—by the number he chose, the God number of school accountability, the cut score.

School ranking systems are simple enough, in theory. Students take tests and the tests are graded. A certain percentage of students will pass, and a certain percentage will fail. The more students who pass, the better a school and its teachers must be.

The simplicity of school accountability as it is popularly understood obscures the intricacy of such a system's moving parts. How hard (or easy) are the test questions? How high (or low) are the passing standards? How high (or low) is the number of passing test-takers needed for a school to be rated effective?

These systems never enjoyed the scrutiny of the scientific method or the purification of honest critique. The most rigorous process they ever went through was a good hashing out by committees of anti-tax businessmen, pro-pandering politicians, and token teachers. It was all pseudoscience, based on truth-like substances and semi-facts instead of actual objective reality.

Meanwhile, the death penalties levied against schools, teachers, and students based on these impure machinations—the condemnations handed out on the basis of these spectral proofs—were very, very real. The erosion of support for teachers was real. The increasing inability of schools to win parents' trust was real. The collapse of partnership between the public and the school in the development of children, as recriminations flew in every direction, was real.

And the scars from these self-inflicted educational wounds will persist for decades.

What Passes for Science

Like the complex algorithms used in educational accountability, the science involved in criminal forensics is mysterious to the layperson, and just as replete with opportunities for error and misuse. If the decisions that rely on school accountability formulas—closing schools, firing teachers, and denying diplomas to kids—are considered high-stakes, then the stakes attached to criminal forensic data are even higher: They are often literally life-and-death.

Michael Morton could speak as fluently as anyone about the misuse of data and the imprudent elevation of pseudoscientific methodologies to prominent and high-stakes roles.

Morton, a former grocery store manager, was charged with murder and sentenced to life in prison following the brutal 1986 slaying of his wife. His guilt was "scientifically proved" by remnants of food found in Christine Morton's stomach during the autopsy, according to the prosecutor who convicted him (Grissom, 2011b). And who can argue with science?

Morton did. He repeatedly requested DNA testing of crime scene evidence. The district attorney's office fought the request tenaciously, claiming that there was no "mystery killer" out there and that Morton was "grasping at straws" (Grissom, 2011a).

In 2010, an appeals court ordered that DNA testing be conducted on a blue bandana found at the crime scene. The test found that hair mixed in with Mrs. Morton's blood on the bandana belonged to a man, but not her husband. It was subsequently matched with the DNA of a felon who had lived up the street from the Morton family at the time of the crime.

After that man's DNA was found at another murder scene, Morton was freed from prison. He had served 25 years for a crime he didn't commit before accurate data finally freed him from a penalty built on a foundation of erroneous data. What saved him was real, objective scientific data, as opposed to the fuzzy facsimile that had convicted him.

"What passes for science in courtrooms is not always, in fact, science," said one advocate for death row inmates in the wake of the Morton decision (Grissom, 2011b).

The Honorable Sid Harle, the judge who dismissed Morton's murder charges, said, "The courts and the sitting judges need to be ever mindful about their role as gatekeeper in regard to the admission of science" (Grissom, 2011b).

Texas state Senator Rodney Ellis was less judicious, calling for "scientific evidence that's based on real science, not some guy saying he has magic dogs that can solve crimes" (Grissom, 2011b).

The misuse of data and testing for high-stakes decisions regarding schools is no less dubious. Nevertheless, governments from coast to coast recklessly bandy about unproven methodologies and employ questionable science to condemn schools, teachers, and students. There is no gatekeeper demanding an honest accounting when it comes to the quality of our kids' schools.

Magic Soap

I can't remember which town it was. I spent so much time going to little Andean communities in the north of Peru that it could've been Chota or Bambamarca, José Galvez or Yanacocha Grande or Yanacocha Chica. I forget where, but what I remember vividly is the open-air market, and in the middle of it, a man standing on a box speaking animatedly into a bullhorn.

Going into rural Andean Peru was like going through a time machine. In Chota the electricity came on for 4 hours a day, and so did the water. In Chinchin Chuquipuquio, the government of Alberto Fujimori had built a new school with light fixtures and porcelain sinks and toilets, anticipating the day—yet to arrive—when electricity and running water would reach the tiny mountain village. In one of the Yanacochas, the men of the town closed and locked a pipe gate across the only road into town at dusk and told my missionary boss and me to go inside and stay there, because the *ronda*—a vigilant mob on horseback, like a Wild West posse but toting machetes instead of Winchesters and wearing ponchos instead of chaps—rode at night and protected the town.

The man on the box seemed like he had stepped right out of America's cowboy days. While I was in Peru to promote Jesus, he was selling magic soap, in a literal sense. I listened in rapt attention as he rattled off a long list of ailments that his soap would cure: AIDS, cancer, *reumatismo*.

I remember the smugness of knowing that as an enlightened American 20-year-old, I was far too smart to fall for such a ruse. These people here could really learn something from us Americans, I told myself.

Looking around today and seeing the men in suits who pitch sketchy metrics and magical education solutions like value-added measures of teacher effectiveness, I realize that we brilliant Americans still have our swindlers. It's just that we've moved them from atop boxes in our open-air markets and into our government buildings.

The VAM Shrapnel Bomb

Value-added measures (VAMs) are purportedly able to tease out the impact, positive or negative, of an individual teacher on student test results, theoretically controlling for outside factors such as poverty and home situations that impact achievement independent of instruction. VAMs are proposed as a basis for teacher firing decisions and decisions regarding which teachers deserve merit pay and which don't. Teacher rankings based on these magical algorithms have been published in major New York and Los Angeles newspapers.

Critics of VAMs argue that "such techniques could be based on shaky assumptions" (Viadero, 2009), which is nothing if not an understatement. VAMs' margins of error are gaping. The average margin of error for value-added measures used in New York City in 2007–2008 was plus or minus 30 points (Di Carlo, 2012). That means a teacher rated in the 50th percentile could in reality be in the 80th percentile, or the 20th. With such imprecision, such a value-added measure provides remarkably useless information. One critic noted that "the estimate for this teacher does not even allow us to have any real confidence that he or she is above or below the median" (Di Carlo, 2012).

Other critics have noted that VAMs are highly unstable. In one study, less than a third of teachers ranked in the top 20% one year were rated as highly the next (Rothstein et al., 2010). Wild fluctuations, in fact, are the norm and not the exception with the first generation of value-added measures. Said one influential team of researchers of the fluctuations: "This runs counter to most people's notions that the true quality of a teacher is likely to change very little over time and raises questions about whether what is measured is largely a 'teacher effect' or the effect of a wide variety of other factors" (Rothstein et al., 2010). Meanwhile, the stated purpose of VAMs is to accurately identify good and bad teachers, not to wildly mislabel legions of people so that we—a significant portion of the time—end up promoting the bad and firing the good in our schools.

But don't tell all that to state superintendents and urban school chiefs who are forging ahead with VAMs. If only these educational thought leaders were as hard on statisticians and technocrats as they are on teachers; if only they similarly insisted on no excuses for the merchants of educational alchemy.

These concerns have led many to urge caution with the use of VAMs. Even staunch VAM advocates are often heard saying things like, "No one suggests using value-added analysis as the sole measure of a teacher" (Strauss, 2011). The only problem with that statement is that it's a lie. Lots of people are suggesting exactly that. Despite the assurances of VAM advocates that this dangerously in-accurate, collateral damage–causing shrapnel bomb of an account-ability tool will be used wisely, the *Los Angeles Times* and *New York Times* each cavalierly published value-added scores for individual teachers, with one LA reporter actually confronting a teacher and convincing her, after she contended that her students did well and parents were pleased with her work, that she was indeed subpar (Strauss, 2011). High-minded concerns about the validity of VAMs or their misuse were nowhere to be found then or when the *New York Post* carried a photo of a teacher of recent immigrants alongside an article identifying her as the "city's worst teacher" (Roberts, 2012).

Contextual Accountability

Every school is a microcosm of the community it serves—that is, ev-ery truly democratic school that serves any and all students in the neighborhood is a microcosm of its community.[2] If there are drugs or violence in the streets, educators will contend with drugs and vio-lence working their way into the school like crickets through unseen cracks. If there are racist or misogynistic attitudes in the homes, they will manifest themselves on campus.

Educators spend entire careers—some without even realizing it—trying to accentuate and play off of students' positive outside influences and minimize or at least sidestep their negative ones, just to prepare the groundwork so they can teach their actual content. Teaching doesn't happen in a vacuum, an obvious fact which bears repeating only because it's so common to hear people go on and on about teacher quality as the ultimate driver of student learning. Too many experts spout the mogul-endorsed "no excuses" mantra re-flexively when the conversation turns to the context of student lives, and in so doing effectively refuse to talk seriously about the increas-ingly horrific conditions of that context.

As though it doesn't matter. As though it needn't be tended to. As though a serious education can occur no matter what is going on there. "Poverty isn't destiny" is trite and ultimately pretends that there is no such phenomenon as generational want.

But poverty is water in the gas tank of education, and its apologists condemn a pit crew of teachers who are pushing sputtering lives, though not fast enough, around a track where youthful suburban rockets whiz by in their mall rat garb.

Teaching is complex. People who talk about it but don't do it every single day fall into a trap of self-congratulatory oversimplification. On a stage or on *Meet the Press*, a series of bumper-sticker phrases may seem to be *right on*— when they are in reality platitudes assembled to construct a virtual reality convincing to well-meaning onlookers and passionate neophytes. However, reform isn't talk; in actual schoolhouses, those doing the work are busy educating rich kids, middle-class kids, poor kids, special education kids, gifted-and-talented kids, and every other kind of kid imaginable; and teachers who take their calling seriously—the majority, I like to think—have never *not* been reforming their practices.

(Yes, it's popular to say schools haven't changed since our agrarian days because we still have summer break. Tell that to 6th-graders in their after-school computer coding club or rural teenagers unleashing rowing-powered machines of their own construction in skits about time travel for a creativity contest. To cling to a convenient belief in overwhelming educational stasis, one has to ignore commonplace things like video production classes, student websites, homework turned in on thumb drives, virtual field trips, blended learning, all manners of creative scheduling, dual-credit academic and vocational courses, podcasts, and dozens of other things no one ever heard of in the 1950s. This particular strain of school-bashing is as logically rigorous as saying cars haven't changed since the 1890s because they still have four wheels.)

The conventional pabulum leaves much to be desired for those of us with dry erase marks on our knuckles. Workaday educators have to discover (through trial and error) the right answers to specific, small-picture questions about curriculum, classroom management, and so many other things. Teaching isn't as easy as it sounds.

And neither is reform.

Improvement in the education of economically disadvantaged American students is certainly necessary. The reformers are right at the beginning of the conversation—academic achievement lags in our poorest schools. But they are consistently wrong about the monolithic cause they advance, and about how to fix it and how bellicose and accusatory to be in the process.

They are at their most wrong and most disingenuous when they proffer exemplar schools and programs and say, "Look here. This is what is possible." Secretary Duncan was factually wrong when he told us that Urban Prep Academy in Chicago was showing us the way; President Obama was demonstrably, disprovably incorrect when he singled out Bruce Randolph School in Denver as a model of "what good schools can do."

I believe fervently that Michelle Rhee and an army of like-minded bad-schools philosophizers will one day look around and see piles where their painstakingly-built sandcastles of reform once stood, and they will know the tragic fame of Ozymandias. Billion-dollar data-sorting systems will be mothballed because of their reckless top-down construction. Value-added algorithms will be tossed in a bin marked "History's Big Dumb Ideas." The mantra "no excuses" will retain all the significance of "Where's the beef?" And teachers will still be teaching, succeeding, and failing all over the country, much as they would have been doing if Michelle Rhee had gone into the foreign service and Bill Gates had invested his considerable wealth and commendable humanitarian ambition in improving law enforcement practices or poultry production.

They are building castles out of sand because they are deliberately ignoring the humanity of both student and teacher. What they are calling "excuses" are really "lives." They are really saying, "No lives." Lessons, yes. Teacher evaluation systems, certainly. Data, of course. But lives—real human idiosyncrasies and foibles and challenges that exist neither inside nor outside the schoolhouse but rather transcend both—those are of necessity left out of the reform equation.

If numbers-and-labels accountability is the way it's going to be for schools then the only appropriate accountability must be contextual. A simple look at test scores—or even the slightly more granular value-added look at test score improvement—is grossly insufficient when one considers the vast differences among schools. Socioeconomic differences, for example, but also school-to-school funding differences and student-selection differences are vitally important in terms of academic achievement–related outcomes. These inputs, however, are recklessly, conspicuously, and consistently left out of otherwise remarkably complicated accountability formulas. Suspiciously, formulas used to rate schools and teachers seem to be impressively comprehensive until you come to variables that indict not educators' actions but the state's policies. Data about funding for schools and social supports, for example, are ignored in accountability, but not because they make no difference in outcomes. Of course they do.

So we must ask the psychometricians to do much, much more; or we must ask them to quit. We must not allow them to burn up our fuel and funding and popular will on moonshots taken with half-right calculations that leave out politically inconvenient variables.

My nephew is studying to be an engineer. He talks about a course in fluid dynamics and leaves me with the impression that engineers use formulas that are accurate to a degree very near perfect. When we build towers and dams and bridges in our country, we rely on measures that don't really allow for error. An engineer can tell you with absolute precision how much water can flow through a pipe of a given size buried at a given angle and pushed by a pump of a given horsepower. Not with 60% accuracy can an engineer tell you this, but with stunning exactitude. Construction is too important of a task to leave variables out of the formulas. With big projects, failure can be catastrophic.

The formation of our children, of course, is far more important in terms of our national well-being than that of our bridges. Formulas whose inaccuracies result in the annual arbitrary firing of several great teachers and the blanket terrorization of many, many more will undoubtedly be as catastrophic for our society as an erroneous building code that guides the construction of hundreds of flawed edifices. If the people who teach our kids are to live and die by a value-added measure, it must be a comprehensive, context-honoring value-added measure. It can't be half-right. That isn't good enough. Per-pupil funding distinctions can't be disregarded. Outside-of-school factors both positive and negative must be figured in.

Until policy mavens provide contextual accountability, the ever-bitterer voices of teachers and their supporters will condemn the flawed formulas, along with all that goes along with them, including heavy-handed personnel tactics, profitable privatization schemes, and cheesy Hollywood anti-teacher porn. And until the psychometricians can come up with formulas that accurately reflect the reality of this amazing thing called education, they won't truly be measuring what they claim to measure—hence the propensity for snow jobs in education reform—and many of us on the receiving end will insist that they themselves add nothing of value.

✪ FOUR ✪

Superteachers, Miracles, and Destructive Idealism

MANUEL AND ANTONIA

MANUEL[1] WAS A KIND-HEARTED 9th-grader when he and his siblings arrived from Mexico. He was a big kid, tall and broad across his shoulders, with a plodding intellect but a heart of gold and a smile that never quit. He was tenaciously happy.

I didn't know a lot about Manuel or his sister Antonia when they showed up in my pull-out ESL class, or about their 1st-grade sister Carla, except that they all smiled a lot and none spoke a word of English. The two teenagers and I got to work immediately.

Neither of the older kids was a quick learner. Manuel was conscientious but academic learning wasn't easy for him. He was decidedly more gearhead than bookworm. Antonia was extremely sensitive, I would learn, and this would make learning a new language a tremendous challenge for her. Manuel had a gift that made language-learning easier: He honestly didn't care what anyone thought of him. He would butcher the language with unrestrained glee, and the ability to do that was a great benefit for him when it came to learning English.

Antonia had me as both her ESL and her Spanish teacher. Her section of Spanish 1 was a small class, with maybe three other girls and a smattering of boys. Unfortunately, one of the girls was Samantha, and Samantha was as proud a redneck as you'll find.

From day one, Samantha was mean to and dismissive of Antonia in a million subtle ways and the occasional unsubtle one.

In Spanish class, the adjective "Mexican" comes up sometimes. "*Día de los muertos* is a Mexican holiday," for example. Or, "*Cacahuate* is the Mexican term for 'peanut.'" Students would tell me, "You should say 'Spanish,' not 'Mexican,'" as though the word were a slur. I would remind them that "Mexican" is not an epithet, and that calling something or someone from Mexico "Spanish" was not an act of kindness but of imprecision.

The way Samantha said it, though, "Mexican" was always an epithet.

"Mes-can," she would say, with a sneer, as if the word tasted bad in her mouth. Deliberately, she said it this way. She said it to put Antonia in her place, to let her know she was less-than, that she wasn't entirely welcome here, wasn't one of us.

When Samantha opened her can of disdain, Antonia surely didn't have any idea what the scrawny blonde girl was saying. Unless she was completely clueless, however, she knew where Samantha's heart was because the sneer was bilingual and the ugly tone of her voice was universal. Samantha didn't like Antonia; Antonia had to know it.

I dressed Samantha down when she said "Mes-can." I can't remember how many times she said it. It may have only been once, for all I remember, or it may have been over and over. I hope I was a better teacher than to have let it go on. At any rate, I remember letting her have it, and her playing dumb.

"That's just how I say it," she protested, with a disingenuous giggle and a flutter of her eyelashes. She wanted me to pretend with her that the slur was an innocent linguistic flourish or an involuntary speech disorder that just *seemed like* racism.

Meanwhile, I sensed that the quiet Mexican girl who never hurt anyone really only wanted to learn English and maybe make a friend or two.

I assumed from the beginning that Antonia and Manuel were poor—you could tell as much by the clothes they wore, by their shoes, and by the way they wore their hair. Their mom drove a series of smoke-belching jalopies that she traded with surprising regularity.

I didn't realize how desperately poor "poor" could get in America until I got to know Antonia and Manuel's situation better. I had been sheltered in a rural cocoon like a middle-class *Little Buddha*, my only ideas about poverty coming from the happy-go-lucky poor of the movies and TV and local news stations' guilt-inspiring soup kitchen coverage during the holidays. I never dreamed that rural poverty could reach the extremes I would see.

One day during my conference period I was sitting in the portable building I shared with the special education teacher, and I heard a knock at the door. I opened it to find a grandmotherly woman holding hands with a barefoot toddler in a ratty T-shirt and a sagging diaper. The woman looked like she had come from church; the toddler looked like a street urchin.

"I found him walking on the shoulder of the highway," she said. She had stopped and picked him up, she explained, because cars zipped up and down that particular roadway at a fast clip. "He doesn't speak English," she said. "I didn't know what to do, so I brought him to you."

I was flattered. People in town thought of me as the guy you take Spanish-speaking children to when you find them lost on the street.

I didn't know who this dirty little boy was. I took him off her hands, thanked her, and walked down to the school office with him.

After some investigation, the principal and I somehow figured out this was Antonia's littlest brother, a fourth sibling. I tried calling Antonia's mom, content that the boss needed my Spanish. She didn't answer. We would have to drive over to Antonia's house to see if Mom was home.

When we pulled up to the house, there was no clunker in the driveway. I scaled the rickety steps onto the porch and knocked on the front door. Nothing. There were a couple of living room windows near me, so I peered inside.

I vividly recall the squalor still today; it was like nothing I'd ever seen. Newspapers and old food wrappers and dirty clothes blanketed the floor. There was no furniture other than a television set connected to an old Nintendo Entertainment System. Both machines sat on the floor, their cables strewn between them.

I was shocked at the sight. I felt immediate sympathy for Antonia and Manuel. My lifelong conservatism uttered unkind thoughts in my brain about the mom's neglect, and I didn't shush it.

Eventually, somehow, the principal and I got the little boy into the arms of his harried mom. She had been out looking for him, if I remember right, and while she was grateful, she seemed genuinely oblivious to the grievousness of her neglect in letting the tyke wander away from home.

The education of Antonia would not end well. She never commanded English and I seriously doubt that she ever passed a standardized test. Each year I gauged the siblings' progress in reading, writing, listening, and speaking English with the TELPAS exam, and each year, I found that they were running their language-learning race in a pool of linguistic molasses.

I readily accept most of the blame. Some will contend that I should accept all of it, which is fine but not very productive. I certainly could have done more, and there are undoubtedly some amazing, no-excuses teachers out there who would have wrung more of themselves out for these kids (and, necessarily, saved less of themselves for their own families) and who perhaps would not have rested until they had gotten Antonia up the ladder to "Intermediate" on TELPAS, or maybe even to "Advanced."

But I couldn't find a way. Maybe I wasn't willing to steal enough of me from my wife. Or maybe I just lacked dedication to the well-being of children who aren't my own, or who aren't my own ethnicity. Maybe, deep down, I'm just that terrible of a human being.

Blame it on what you will, I failed with those three. It wasn't because of any negation of the importance of the task. I knew each day that I was trying to give them a fighting chance, to put them on a path to a better life. Maybe I was too lazy. Maybe I was more interested in my own wants than in the needs of those kids. That's the easy knock on traditional teachers in traditional public schools. We just don't have the missionary zeal we need in order to make a positive difference in the world. We are too busy "defending the status quo" to save these kids from the pitfalls inherent in their portion.

I left that school after working with those siblings for 3 or 4 years. After I left, I would see Manuel from time to time, always, it seemed, in Wal-Mart. His English came along gradually, and I remember being impressed the last time he spoke to me. He was probably "Advanced" on the TELPAS, I thought, though he had needed more than the 3 years the state of Texas arbitrarily gave him to get there.

But Antonia didn't have as much time as Manuel. Six months before I left the school, she disappeared from our rolls. I imagine Samantha had a private celebration when she heard Antonia was gone and wasn't coming back. It was almost certainly Samantha who propelled the ugly rumors that Antonia was shipped back to "Mes-co" by her mom after a big fight.

After I heard she was gone, I thought about the time Antonia and I had argued in ESL class about whether *chupacabras* was real. I had been teaching about some American myth or another and had compared it to the Mexican goat-sucking cryptid, and she had gotten visibly mad at me. *Chupacabras* was real; there was one stuffed and mounted in the national museum in Mexico City, she vowed, injured by my unbelief. I finally acquiesced. "Yes, okay," I had laughed. "I believe you."

I never saw Antonia again, and I don't know what became of her. I know there's a good chance that there's no high school diploma from either the United States or Mexico hanging on her wall.

I also know this: I failed to be Superman for her. My experience lives on as a touchstone for me, a reminder of my own educational impotence in the face of great human challenges. As the horsemen of the modern school reform movement actively comb the earth looking for people to blame for the condition of our poorest citizens, here I am. I could be their poster child.

The "failing American public school system" they eagerly speak of is really just a conglomeration of a hundred thousand individual human failures like me.

The great hope of the family, Manuel, died at 19 or 20 when he was electrocuted while working on the electric supply to his home. He had managed to graduate high school. I wonder about the littlest brother, the toddler who had wandered along the shoulder of the highway in his diaper. I hope he ran across his Superman somewhere along the way.

I don't offer this catalogue of a family's personal travails to excuse my failure with Antonia. Ideally, I would have had her speaking fluent academic English within 3 years as the state of Texas demanded. Ideally.

But I never had the luxury of working with ideals. I was too busy managing the messy real.

Three Choices

At some point, education reformers stopped asking teachers to be accountable for quality teaching and started asking them to be accountable for miracles. The film *Waiting for "Superman"* perfectly encapsulated the mythos of "all things are possible" education. Here was Geoffrey Canada nobly creating the Harlem Children's Zone, an area dedicated to children that wrapped them in all the social supports and high expectations needed for them to succeed. The buzz around the movie focused on the bright possibilities it illuminated and largely ignored the massive infusion of costly social supports that made success happen there. It also ignored the seriously narrative-compromising fact that Canada once kicked out an entire class of kids who weren't getting high-enough scores on their tests (Kerchner, 2010).

America wanted the results of the Harlem Children's Zone, but without the unmentioned price tag and without the secret wholesale kicking out of unwanted children. What would that take? Simple. All America needed was a population of teachers who could instruct ably and also singlehandedly overcome the unbridled social devastation faced by America's most at-risk kids.

In short, superteachers were the shorthand answer to America's most intractable problems.

Policymakers, journalists, and think tank wonks embraced the pursuit of superteachers as the way to fix schools and, *ipso facto*, society. This was a destructive idealism, and it spawned all sorts of perversions as the people in the system contorted to find a way to become Supermen and -women, or, in the absence of an ability to pull off the heroics called for by movers and shakers and policymakers, to at least *appear to be* Supermen and -women.

The destructive idealism of miracle-demanding education reform left teachers with no good choices. The demand for miracles trickled down to them from administrators who either arrogantly ("Of course I can do this") or recklessly ("I don't know if I can do it, but I'm going to tell them what they want to hear") assured constituents that they could certainly squeeze amazing academic achievement out of their students, no problem. No matter what circumstances the children found themselves in, these administrators weren't about to make any excuses. If Geoffrey Canada could do it, of course they could too. No money? No problem. If these child-saving administrators had to beat their teachers with sticks to make it happen, all children could and would learn. They just cared that much about children.

Poverty schmoverty. You won't find any soft bigotry here.

And so the school reform movement veered bizarrely into a miracle movement. Nationally recognized superintendents and pundits took upon themselves the rhetorical trappings of faith healers. They traded TV preachers' claims of "if your faith is strong enough" with the educational faith statement of "if you care enough" and assured everyone that anything is possible. Education reform became the prosperity gospel of schools. We could name it and claim it. If we could conceive it, we could achieve it. What we treasured, we would measure.

Just as faith without labor could make believers in the prosperity gospel rich, so too were learning miracles possible in schools where academic priests held aloft the promise of genius without books, bricks without straw, and lush intellectual humanity without parks or reflection or well-appointed libraries. There was no need to address social injustice or horrific home conditions: Even bringing those up, we were told, would let teachers off the hook and constituted adult-centered excuse-making. In this twisted worldview, the radical compassion of thinkers like Jonathan Kozol somehow came to be viewed as wicked and selfish.

In reality, the education reform movement—much like the prosperity gospel movement—amounted to little more than a multilevel marketing scheme. The people at the top, the most willing to tell tall tales and hook in followers, enriched themselves, and they left the suckers at the bottom holding the bag.

The moment miracles became the goal in education, non-superhero teachers (who nonetheless aimed to please) were torn. They were forced to choose among the improbability of actually performing miracles on a consistent basis, the personal devastation of falling short of expectations, and the great moral failure of cheating.

Who are these people who become teachers? In my experience, a significant percentage are people who liked school and who almost never failed or cheated; who, in fact, generally have a visceral revulsion to failing and an even more visceral revulsion to cheating. Yet the system we built in the furtherance of the noble, impossible goal of getting ravaged kids to perform just as well as nurtured kids on achievement tests—without spending too much on social supports—left teachers only three choices, all of them bad: *perform miracles, fail, or cheat.*

When miracles became the goal, cheating became a currency. Some of it happened at the top, as when, at the dawn of the movement, administrators in Houston reportedly fudged their dropout numbers, or more recently when central administrators in El Paso allegedly shuffled strugglers out of grades required to test for federal accountability. Cheating at this level was a highly refined Enron-style number-cruncher gaming of the system, rather than the traditional "let me see your answers" kind of cheating we tend to associate with schools. But there was plenty of that going on as well. Outside the central offices, teachers and principals in Atlanta were indicted for systematically changing wrong student answers to right answers on testing sheets. According to allegations that no one but John Merrow has been willing to investigate with seriousness, the same thing happened in Washington, DC, under the leadership of education reform heroine Michelle Rhee.

Manufacturing Marvels

I can't say that I've never been tempted. Career-wise, there was plenty at stake. As a principal helping to stack and sort answer documents and test booklets to mail back to the corporation that would score them, I had plenty of opportunities to cheat. We all did, and still do. I probably could've gotten away with it. It's fun to imagine how my superintendent might have reacted if my scores climbed steadily to unrivaled heights during my tenure. I love kudos. I never got many kudos as a campus principal because if my scores rose (and I honestly don't remember if they did), they didn't rise dramatically. I didn't eat any bees, and I didn't perform any miracles. What I performed—and am defiantly proud of—was a daily slog of non-miraculous educational feats: things like creating a positive climate, relating authentically to kids and parents and staff, and other boring old stuff that just isn't trendy among the cognoscenti nowadays. Nothing flashy, just consistent.

If I had performed (or fabricated) a miracle, I could have presented at conferences. I could have written papers. I could have attributed the rise in scores to the mandatory enrichment program that my peers and I developed. We could've trademarked that. I could've sold that story, could've packaged it as a program. I could've told everyone I had discovered the elixir.

I wouldn't have changed just any kids' papers, either. No, I would've gone straight for the kids who hit us multiple times on the accountability system: a limited English proficient student who is also Hispanic and learning disabled, for example. More bang for your buck there: You can get a three-for-one deal if you pass a student who inhabits multiple subpopulations, who might have been a hit or a miss on his own. I could have just nudged the odds a bit with two or three little imperceptible changes. I will say here that I never came close to cheating. I don't care about this career that much.

On the other hand, I didn't work in one of the most challenging urban schools in the nation, and I didn't work under a hyperambitious superintendent who exerted copious pressure on me to make gains at any cost. I had a prayer of meeting minimum state expectations, though it certainly wasn't guaranteed. Beyond that, I had the notion that even if I didn't meet the standard, I wouldn't likely be fired on the spot. I was confident I would have a chance to fix the problem if the scores came back wanting.

Cheating is currency in this era of miracle-demanding, excuse-eschewing educational accountability, but it's a currency most educators can't bring themselves to trade in. Those who reject cheating, then, are left with only two options. They must either become miracle-makers or embrace failure. (I suppose there is one other option: A teacher could find a job teaching in the suburbs, where miracles often aren't required to get kids to pass these tests.)

I have no idea how many principals and teachers—folks whose jobs are on the line over these numbers—have cheated over the years. I assume it's about the same proportion as those who fudge on their taxes. After all, neither is more or less ethical than the other, nor more or less obviously harmful to society. Yes, we have high hopes for our teachers; we believe they should be the most ethical among us. And they probably are. But they're human.

Much has been written about teachers and administrators who cheat on accountability. Reformers typically declare that these stories indicate moral failings on the part of individuals, and that the tests and the stakes shouldn't be blamed for the sins of flawed people. Critics of punitive accountability argue that the pressures applied to teachers in America's hardest-hit, poorest neighborhoods is untenable and drives desperate educators to do unthinkable things.

But little is written about another kind of cheating that happens away from the schoolhouse. The corporate testing community has cheated taxpayers over and over by delivering subpar test items, launching glitch-prone online exams, misgrading tests and mistakenly labeling children who pass as failures, and overcharging states to the tune of millions of dollars. The media gets in on the cheating when journalists paper over the misdeeds of testing companies and bury reports of testing errors on the back page, or fail to report them altogether. Worse, the media has extolled a panoply of miracle schools and miracle educators whose wonders have proven to be fraudulent; only in rare cases—John Merrow comes to mind—have retractions or re-examinations been issued.

And politicians cheat in a very literal sense every time they crib model legislation from organizations whose members include testing companies and turn them in as their own work, presenting them as bills they "authored" in their respective statehouses. They cheat democracy itself by proposing laws that serve the brazen fiscal interests of standardized test sellers over the educational interests of American children. Together, testing companies, reporters, and politicians conspire to convince the public that the systems built on the tests are objective and tell unassailable truths about our children and our schools. This is a greater conspiracy than any cheating ring, with much greater rewards at stake.

Shouldn't they be held accountable too?

Mandatory Miracles

Many of our teachers and principals are people-pleasers. Accountability for miracles leaves them with diabolically limited options: Do they cheat or do they fail?

Idealistic reformers will, of course, point to another, more inspiring, alternative: The teachers could simply perform the miracles the nation insists on. These idealists have never actually performed academic miracles themselves, mind you, but they assure the nation that it's possible. Some, like Michelle Rhee, claim to have worked academic astonishments, but objective evidence is hard to come by. This fact matters little, though, because America is in such dire need of miracles.

We don't have time to wait to verify that these magic pills work; we just have to hurry and swallow them. Our public school teachers could—if they just cared enough—become the inner-city superheroes we need them to be and consistently produce results on par with elite private schools; they could cling to excellence and innovation and efficiency and *just make it happen*. They could quit whining and, with enough top-down pressure, simply figure out how to pull it off. America desperately needs them to turn lead into gold, to turn water into wine, and America has heard and believed that there are some really excellent and innovative ways to do those things. The people purporting to do them are superstars, and they endlessly tout their miracles and sell their mystery compounds.

The idealists try madly to find miracles to point to as exemplars of what is possible, so that faithless realists will be shamed and silenced. KIPP charter schools and Harlem Children's Zone are doing it, they say. Why can't the public schools? They find and promote miracles in order to convince our teachers that they too can turn social devastation into academic achievement, if they only try really hard and don't make excuses.

This mindset implies that the accountability gods keep a passion scale rigged up to a miracle trigger on Mount Achievement. Urban Prep becomes the Virgin of Urban Prep. Steve Perry becomes Saint Steve. Michelle Rhee cries crocodile tears of blood for the children, and we teachers all believe with all of our hearts that we too can perform miracles.

And we all self-loathe when we don't. (Almost always, we don't.)

Ultimately, under critical examination, the miracle schools invariably dissolve into mundane and uninspiring reconfigurations of our age-old educational setup, with a few modern tricks employed to juice the numbers. Some use attrition or high standards or stringent parent contracts to shoo away the kids who are immune to miracles. (Who needs excuses when you can have expulsions?) Some spend eye-popping amounts of money on social supports that lawmakers will never approve at scale. Some cheat. Some probably do all three. In all cases, reform cheerleaders regularly deign to compare those schools to traditional schools as though all things are equal.

Meanwhile, some very good schools have achieved laudable results with little fanfare by steadfastly implementing traditional approaches typically spurned by modern education thinkers. Many strategies found in these exceptional "non-miracle schools" are associated with a classic democratic education philosophy that has been summarily rejected by reformers: small class sizes, universal prekindergarten, and equity of treatment, to name a few of the strategies.

One school district of this kind is in Union City, New Jersey, where the unemployment rate dwarfs that of the rest of the nation and a large majority of the students are from homes in which English is not a native language (Kirp, 2013). The story of this surprising school district is told in the book *Improbable Scholars*, written by UC Berkeley professor David Kirp.

Schools like Union City are typically not canonized as miracle schools by the reform crowd, as their results weren't sudden and incredible enough, and they weren't attributed to a rather specific set of methodologies persistently pushed by reformers. Instead, the positive changes in such schools are described as gradual and sustained. Such schools offer "nothing earthshaking," to quote the author, but still achieve great success for children (Kirp, 2013). Union City saw 75% of its 2012 graduates enroll in college, for example (Kirp, 2013).

Kirp described the inspiring story of these schools as "tortoise beats hare" (2013).

But unlike Union City, the miracle schools that make reform news are flashy. Their results sometimes strain credulity, as when the Houston Independent School District posted a 0% dropout rate in a number of its crowded high schools before a whistleblower blew the lid off the fraud (Winerip, 2003). Then there are the claims of so-called 90/90/90 schools—schools with 90% poverty, 90% minority populations, and 90% passing rates on standardized tests. A blogger named Gary Rubinstein has made a hobby out of debunking such breathless claims.

Here is Rubinstein's take on one school that President Barack Obama offered as evidence of the miracle schools gospel: "Obama praised Denver's Bruce Randolph school because 97% of their 50 seniors graduated. He failed to mention that there were 100 freshmen three years earlier" (Rubinstein, 2011).

No matter where one looks, if one looks closely enough, so-called miracle schools appear to sift kids at the doors, to find ways to cheat on the tests or finagle the data, or burn through people trying to become what teachers and principals should never have been asked to be in the first place: poverty-killers.

Mandatory miracles make for dumb public policy. This kind of wishful thinking harms kids by withholding from them a realistic, methodical approach to improvement.

"Overwhelmed, Underappreciated, and Underpaid"

Steven Brill, author of a book about education called *Class Warfare*, is a big fan of neoliberal education policy. In his book he celebrates many of the touchstones of modern education reform. He is enamored of the idea of young, idealistic, Ivy League graduates who bravely enter the mission fields of inner-city schools and save poor Black kids from themselves. Brill appears to believe that great teaching alone can overcome the challenges that systematically confound our nation's most struggling schools: poverty, apathy, and inadequate parenting. Brill is a fan of no-excuses charter schools.

As Brill wrote glowingly about one such school in New York City—and not so glowingly about the traditional public school that met in the same building—he discovered an inspiring young lady named Jessica Reid. Reid was a no-excuses educator whom Brill described as "the most stubborn person who you will ever meet" (Thompson, 2011).

Reid was one of the people whom Brill calls "the heroes of the charter-school movement" (Brill, 2011). The villains are "teachers' union leaders and education bureaucrats who, for 4 decades, have presided over schools that provide comfortable public jobs for the adults who work there but wretched instruction for the children who are supposed to learn there" (Brill, 2011).

Brill gets credit for confronting the working conditions faced by non-unionized teachers in "miracle" charter schools. "I feel overwhelmed, underappreciated, and underpaid," said one such teacher. And "there is no way I can do this beyond another year or two," said another (Brill, 2011).

Jessica Reid wasn't a teacher when Brill showed up at her school. She had been a teacher, but she was so passionate, so dedicated, and so successful that she had been promoted to assistant principal at 28 years of age. In one interview with Brill, Reid said, "I know I can't do this forever. And I know if I had a child I couldn't do it. As it is, it is screwing up my marriage" (Brill, 2011).

Reid made those comments on a Wednesday. Four days later, Brill learned that she had resigned her six figure job. Reid, Brill reported, was "a truly gifted educator," but she reported to him in the months after her resignation that what she did day after day in the miracle school "wasn't a sustainable life, in terms of my health and my marriage" (Brill, 2011).

Sadly, Brill's writing drips with subtle contempt for people like me and my three sisters and my best friend from childhood—all of us teachers who probably fall somewhere short of "truly gifted" on Brill's Scale of Eager Classroom Martyrdom. We fall short because, whereas Reid said "you can never sit down," we occasionally do (Brill, 2011). We aren't—and I'm biased—bad teachers. We don't offer "wretched instruction" (Brill, 2011). But I would venture that none of us is committed enough to the academic achievement of other people's children that we would jeopardize our marriages or our health in favor of some constructed virtue like workaholism. At the risk of speaking for my siblings and my best friend, I'll offer that we don't pretend to be martyrs.

We are teachers, nothing more and nothing less. In my opinion at least, that is more than enough to merit a small measure of appreciation.

The rhetoric of today has us pegged as defenders of the status quo and cheerleaders for mediocrity. I believe, instead, that we are defenders of an approach to teaching children that ensures a lifelong impact. Are we trying to make it to our pensions? You bet. Does that deal—stick with this career long enough and you get to retire on enough money to not starve in your old age—benefit society, or does it benefit only us?

Ask our students, not Steve Brill.

As (I think) a fair-minded person who has worked alongside many teachers who stayed in the classroom for three and four decades, I have trouble with the hinted-at notion that they're sandbagging and dispassionate because they didn't burn out after a couple of years. I'm left with a nagging question: Who is a better teacher—the sprinter who totally pours himself or herself out for 5 years or less, or the marathoner who paces himself or herself and makes a steady, sustainable commitment to children's well-being for 30 years? The hare, or the tortoise?

The spokespeople for school reform often talk about schools in stark terms, as if you have Jessica Reids on the one hand and rubber room teachers on the other; heroes and villains, in Brill's parlance.

I find that the reality of school is far less binary. You can't sell books and policy proposals talking about merely "decent teachers" or "good teachers" or "solid and consistent teachers." They must be either remarkably good or remarkably bad, or else why remark on them? They have to be great or miserable.

The reality that there aren't two extremes of teacher quality is inconvenient for those who market ideologies, but it's true. There is an infinitely fine spectrum of teacher quality, and the spectrum spans out in eleven dimensions. Ms. Jones is really good at relating to kiddoes, but her classroom management is shaky. Mr. Smith is amazingly committed and works long hours, but he is brusque and awkward and many kids don't connect with him. Ms. Adams knows her subject and doesn't let kids leave her room without learning a ton, but she beats the buses out of the parking lot at the end of the day (and I've heard she stops for a margarita on the way home 4 days a week).

School reform asks no teachers to be bad, but it also effectively demands that no teachers be simply good. The rhetoric insists that all teachers be superteachers.

If we asked all our soldiers to be Green Berets, we wouldn't have enough enlisted to fight a war. The same is true of teachers.

The fight for academic excellence is a breeze in some neighborhoods, a chore in others, and a desperate war in still others. There are 3 million teachers in America. As in any profession, some are passionate believers in the mission of the organization and some are there to collect a paycheck. Should all of them be passionate and selfless? Yes, just as all salespeople should sell their products because they truly believe in their usefulness and quality. But, alas, some salespeople just want to sell because they have a family to provide for, and some teachers are not aiming for miracles but for retirement.

Similarly, some folks in the Army are just trying to get to the end of their enlistments. It's great that we celebrate and make movies about Green Berets, but I'm thankful we don't tear down every soldier who isn't one. We don't need Green Berets stationed in the easy places. We don't need every member of the Navy to qualify for Seal Team Six.

I will most likely end my career never having attempted to teach in one of the poorest neighborhoods in America. I recognize this means I'll never have an uplifting movie made about my teaching career—"rural White kid grows up and teaches rural White kids" wouldn't make for a mesmerizing tale, exactly.

I'm not a Green Beret of teaching. I'm a grunt. If I were single, maybe I'd go into the miracle fields, but I chose to raise a family and live near to where I grew up. In terms of educational heroism, I'm something like an Army typist. I have nothing but respect for the Jessica Reids of the world. We could always use more passionate, save-the-world educators.

But I also have immeasurable respect for Coach and Mrs. Hart. She was my first mentor, and he was her husband. A "floater," I taught my very first high school class in her room during her conference. She encouraged me to hold the kids accountable, to take the job seriously, not to be a wimp, and to be their teacher, not their buddy. She was a demanding teacher and a really good one. She commanded the respect of the entire community and propelled who knows how many students on to college. But she was no martyr. She and her husband took trips in their RV over spring break, and I seriously doubt she gave kids her cell phone number and offered to help them with homework while she was away.

My gut feeling—with no disrespect meant toward the indefatigable Jessica Reid—is that Mrs. Hart did as much good for America, and America's children, as Reid. She wasn't a miracle teacher in a miracle school. She was a committed teacher in a community school, and she was that for 4 decades. Her non-miraculous but persistently positive results garnered compound interest over time. She taught multiple generations of many families. She didn't make kids maintain eye contact like they do in some high-performing schools for all 40 of her years, but she did make kids sit up and listen and complete their assignments. She didn't repeat miracle scripts and power words and platitudes, but she pushed doggedly for kids to get serious about their learning.

She fought the good fight.

She also sat down once in a while.

FIVE

The Educational Dark Ages I: Ignorance

MY FAVORITE PART OF Ms. Snyder's high school biology class was when we learned about biological classification. I had heard of *homo sapiens* for years, but until we started studying genera and phyla and orders and families, I didn't really understand what it meant. I was (and still am) awed by the notion that basically every living thing—every plant and animal and microscopic life form—has been classified using a sensible rationale. And I was not only awed; as an adolescent terrified by the emergent complexity of impending adulthood, I was calmed by the order Ms. Snyder showed us. I would get that same relief—it all *fits*, it all makes sense—when we studied the periodic table of elements in her chemistry class.

White Hats and Black Hats

Thanks in part to Ms. Snyder, I believe there is a natural taxonomy of practically everything if we will just analyze our surroundings as thoughtfully as Carolus Linnaeus or Dmitri Mendeleev. When it comes to the kingdom of modern school reform, I believe we can sort the membership into at least two phyla: white hat reformers and black hat reformers. The white hat reformers insist on radical change to the public education system in America out of a sincere belief that the current system has failed the most vulnerable children in our society. These are passionate, kind-hearted people with noble intent. When they bare their teeth, it's because they believe adults are looking out for their own interests over those of vulnerable children who've been neglected by our unfair society. It's understandable, though I can't say I have enjoyed being on the receiving end of some of their more unkind blanket arguments.

These fiercely compassionate souls seek levers—often free market ideas like school vouchers—to force rapid and dramatic improvements, especially in inner-city schooling.

Black hat reformers are different. These folks have ulterior motives. They are in it not truly for the children but have embraced reform either for the money or for the votes. In some cases, they are merely in it to advance a political point of view, and schools are just the latest battlefield.

White hat reformers are not motivated by profit or ideology, but by compassion.

Sadly, their compassion doesn't always extend to the adults who labor in schools on behalf of the children under remarkably trying conditions. They often embrace a rule we might call zero-sum compassion: Any compassion shown to educators is compassion stolen from schoolchildren. Under this scenario, the properly compassionate person must reserve all of his or her compassion for the helpless kids and none for their teachers.

But this scenario is wrong.

"Stunted Morale"

From my perspective as an administrator at a fairly typical rural school, teaching in the American K–12 education system has become more daunting than ever before. I would guess that, with fewer kids dropping out, more special needs students in mainstream classrooms, and soaring learning expectations, growth in the challenge of teaching has outpaced growth in the buying power of teachers' paychecks. In these austere times, merit pay has been offered as a way to obtain raises for some teachers, but there may well be a greater number of meritorious teachers in America than there is funding for merit pay.

All three of my children have great, nurturing, engaging teachers as of this writing. Predictably, all three have at one time or another this year expressed an interest in becoming a teacher themselves. Though my wife and I and all of my siblings are educators, I must admit that my response was swift and decisive: Don't do it.

Many American students are hard to teach. Maybe it's always been this challenging; in 1983, teachers surveyed for one study identified disinterested students and parents as the top two problems in education (Bishop, 1989). Overcoming student apathy is not a new challenge, then, for teachers. American teenagers were probably never overly excited about schoolwork. What has changed is the unfailing expectation that teachers will inspire even the most disengaged pupil and get them college-ready by the time they graduate. The prevailing mentality among education watchers is akin to expecting doctors to ensure that their patients universally—including the most critically ill among them—don't merely survive, but get well enough to run a triathlon while under their care. High expectations have replaced personalized care in the American secondary classroom. All children can and must scale Mount College Readiness, even the ones who can't and don't want to.

Once, it was heroism enough to take a student who didn't want to be in school and convince her to stick it out and graduate. In today's no-excuses reality, however, there are no pats on the back for the kid who crawls across the finish line or for the teacher who kept him from spitting out disgusted profanities and walking away from schooling halfway through the race. Even kids with the most daunting of personal challenges—sexual abuse, incarcerated or absentee parents, foodlessness, homelessness, social isolation, impoverished circumstances—are allotted no excuses and—it's well-meaning, I suppose—are effectively discouraged by policy from "lowering their sights" and learning a well-paying and marketable trade like plumbing or computer programming. Any victory in a child's life that falls short of college entrance is no longer celebrated as a victory. Schooling in America has become a track team in which even burly shot-putters and lanky high-jumpers are expected to run on the sprint team; their particular strengths go unacknowledged and the tasks to which they are uniquely suited and in which they are uniquely interested are dismissed as unworthy of training and outside the auspices of valid pursuit.

When the conversation turns to the dire conditions of inner-city pupils, socially conscious public schools advocates are often shushed by those who are hesitant to allow poverty to be an excuse for ineffective instructional practices or what President Bush referred to as "the soft bigotry of low expectations" ("Transcript of," n.d.). A common rebuttal to concerns raised about the fact that the United States has one of the highest rates of child poverty among developed countries is the contention that large numbers of children in academically high-performing Asian nations also live in financially poor conditions. "Low national income does not necessarily signify poor educational performance," read one report about 2009 international test scores (Armario, 2010).

This argument is in turn often met with a claim that poverty in America is more corrosive to aspiration-driven tasks like learning because it exists within the brutal context of a gaping inequality of income. As Max Fisher noted in the *Washington Post*, "the U.S. economy is one of the most unequal in the developed world. This would explain why the United States, on child poverty, is ranked between Bulgaria and Romania, though Americans are on average six times richer than Bulgarians and Romanians" (Fisher, 2013).

The argument is this: It isn't that our inner-city kids are poor and poor kids can't learn; the problem is that our poor inner-city children are surrounded by an apparatus of unfairness that serves as an apparent near-guarantor of their station in life. Why work hard in school if the system is against you?

Poor children can indeed learn. But the question is, in a system eaten to shreds by inequity and callous injustice, can they hope? The hopeless do not study.

Anecdotally, I can report that we have come to a place in America where too many students disrespect themselves, their teachers, and education itself, and we simplistically respond by damning our teachers for the results of what we've all together—as a nation, not merely as an educational system—allowed our kids to become.

Declining commitment to learning among students and the apparent decrease in parental support for learning aren't the only challenges facing teachers. Not by a long shot. A 2012 Gates Foundation/Scholastic survey of teachers reported a litany of complaints in the teachers' own words:

- I spend half my day disciplining students.
- Budget cuts mean my prep time is gone, which means I can't learn or collaborate with my colleagues.
- I have too much paperwork and not enough time to spend with my students.
- I need adequate supplies and technology.
- How can we see progress if we keep changing our plans?
- Smaller class size would allow me to differentiate instruction.
- [Students'] lives shouldn't depend on them [standardized tests], and neither should ours.
- The obsession with student performance on standardized tests is forcing me to teach only the content that will be covered on that test.
- The amount of time spent preparing for testing is disgraceful. (Primary Sources, 2012)

According to a poll of teachers taken in 2011 by MetLife, "the number of teachers who reported they were 'very satisfied' dropped by 15 points between 2009 and 2011, from 59 to 44 percent" (Resmovitz, 2012). In an article about these two teacher surveys, one author noted: "while the goal of education is not to please teachers, stunted morale hurts. The entire enterprise of education depends on the relationship between a child and the person responsible for facilitating learning" (Resmovitz, 2012).

Besides the specific difficulties that arise day to day in the work life of a teacher, there is another, more overarching issue that may be more generally corrosive to the attractiveness of the job than any other complaint: the lack of esteem in the public square. When I started teaching, I had it in my head that teachers were viewed positively by the public at large. The profession, at least in my mind, was associated with other heroic callings to public service. I was in a league with police officers, paramedics, soldiers, and firefighters like my father. I was a sacrificial giver doing good in my society.

I was wrong. I don't know that I was necessarily wrong *at that time*, but if not, then the public perception of teachers appears to have changed drastically over the course of my career. Public opinion about me and my occupation seems to have shifted for the worse. A strain of rhetoric is out there—and maybe it always was and I just didn't know it—that paints teachers as takers. We are viewed in some quarters, astoundingly, as members of a selfish profession.

One reporter shared the impression of a teacher this way:

> [Beth] Sanders . . . knew that long hours and challenging circumstances were part of the job description when she signed up to teach. But now, on top of all her responsibilities, she has to answer to critics who judge her work according to the high-performance rhetoric proliferated by policymakers. She says she's sick of being evaluated by people who know nothing about her job. (Resmovitz, 2012)

K–12 schooling in America is going through a kind of educational dark age, a time in which well-meaning missionaries of high expectations are loading up on barques and crashing into the shorelines of the public schools continent. By necessity, they sail alongside swaggering ignoramuses who have promised distant benefactors that they will find El Dorado in education and return with a bounty. It's a symbiotic relationship: The profiteers need to seem benevolent, so the well-intentioned zealots give them cover; and the zealots need a sponsor for their proselytizing, so the profiteers oblige.

Teachers are indigenous here—they are the village elders who grew up in the tribes—and the missionaries' only goal is to win them over to the religion of no excuses.

These are the well-meaning school reformers, the white hats, the ones who visit our inner-city schools and recoil at what they see.

They are kind, but they are nonetheless ignorant, and in their ignorance they often judge quickly and harshly. They oversimplify. They demonize when they should differentiate. They are clearly much better human beings than the Francisco Pizarros sent in to pillage the system for financial gain, but they do no less damage. Just as priests killed many more Indians with smallpox than the *conquistadores* did with swords, so too the white hat reformers today—like the Teach for America intern who posted "we are younger, more energetic, and better than the older teachers in our building"—are apt, in the interest of being radical for the children, to pour boiling oil over the heads of the natives when they don't convert quickly enough to the one true religion of no-excuses reform (Rubinstein, 2011).

CHINCHIN TRES CRUCES

I WAS A SEMI-MISSIONARY. I know what it's like to show up in a new place where everything is different, and to do so with good intentions but to simultaneously be ignorant of my own biases, to be unaware of my penchant for running everyone and everything through my ever-present cultural filter. I meant to go to Peru to share the light of Jesus. Unwittingly, though, I carried with me the pall of a raging cluelessness that I was not a savior but a bumbling, not-so-humble outsider.

Kody Allen was over six feet tall; he was lean and fit and in his forties. Kody was what they call a "church planter," who, with his wife, was responsible for getting new Baptist churches up and running in the international mission field.

I admired missionaries as a kid. We had classes at church called Mission Friends on Wednesday nights. We studied these people; we read about their adventures. They were like Indiana Jones, but with Bibles.

I liked working with Kody Allen. He had been a Golden Gloves boxer. He was the only Southern Baptist I had ever met who wasn't from the South. He was from New Jersey. He and I shared a love for the writings of C. S. Lewis.

Kody and I worked together to get a Baptist church off the ground in Chinchin Chuquipuquio. Another mission project led by a crusty old Texan with a worn-out drilling rig and the least-wholesome vocabulary of any missionary I ever met had punched a hole in the middle of the village, and Kody's job was to follow up the water well with a church plant. The people of Chinchin Chuquipuquio would thirst no more.

Chinchin Chuquipuquio was my village. Kody had entrusted it to me, and I drove up and led church services there once a week. Kody came from time to time to make sure I wasn't teaching these people to worship Mother Earth or something.

So on this one Sunday night, Kody and I made the 2-hour trip up the mountain in his shiny Toyota instead of my old raggedy one, and we spent 2 or 3 hours with the *campesinos* singing songs accompanied by their boisterous drum and guitars. We made a joyful noise in the style of the upbeat *huaynos* that the Andean Indians played on their battery-powered radios. We probably fired up the generator and projected some outdated Christian film after the singing and Kody's sermon.

When it was over, the men of the village stood around the Toyota with Kody and me, and we talked. The stars were always amazing up there, miles away from light pollution, sparkling on the other side of a clear mountain sky. And on this particular night, there was an eclipse.

We talked about the eclipse and the beauty of the innumerable stars and, mandatorily, the glory of God; we reaffirmed each other's sacred hopes, a thing which is pleasant even now to remember, and we lingered there.

It was midnight when we finally broke the peace of that night by clambering into the truck and slamming the doors. The men of the village said their long goodbyes and so did we, and Kody slid the four-by-four into gear.

We bumped down the mountain alternating between small talk and pensive silence until we came to the only town between Chinchin Chuquipuquio and the city. Chinchin Tres Cruces barely passed for a town. It was really a smattering of adobe houses strewn across the undulating mountains, with *chacras*—corn fields—surrounding them. Only one of the dozen or so houses was anywhere close to the gravel road we were rumbling down. It stood just off the shoulder, on the downhill side of the road. On the uphill side a corn field with tall shadowy stalks sloped up and away from the small bluff where the road had been cut into the mountain.

"What?" Kody muttered. I peered ahead to see what he saw. Strangely, at some time between midnight and 1:00 in the morning, a mother and her five or six children were standing in a line in front of the house by the road as if they were waiting for a bus to pick them up.

The smallest of the children was a toddler with a tiny poncho and straw hat. The oldest was maybe 12.

It was the oldest who caught Kody's eye as our headlights illuminated the scene.

"Don't even think about it," Kody muttered.

The preteen was holding a rock in his hand the way a kid might hold a skipping stone, his index finger curled around the stone's edge and his arm bouncing slightly as if he were weighing it, readying his lean muscles for a launch.

"Don't you do it," Kody hissed, and our truck bounced by in front of the family.

I saw the boy draw back his arm out of the corner of my eye. The ping of the stone hitting my passenger-side door reverberated straight into Kody's ear, and Kody went blind with offense.

The missionary stomped the brake and the blue Toyota ground to a halt in the middle of the empty gravel road. At midnight. Miles from anywhere.

The stone thrower disappeared before Kody could get to the mom.

"¿Dónde está el niño?" Kody demanded of the lady. He was a foot and a half taller than her.

"¿Dónde está?" The *campesina* didn't know what he was talking about. What boy? What stone?

I left the truck without really wanting to. I was convinced this was a bad idea, but I figured my boss would remember it if I didn't at least get out. As soon as my feet hit the ground, two scrawny mutts began nipping at my pant legs.

As Kody grew more agitated and the woman persisted in her feigned ignorance, I noticed movement behind the missionary. A man appeared from the shadows behind the adobe house. Not much taller than the woman I assumed was his wife, he slipped closer to my unsuspecting boss, tossed his crimson poncho over his shoulder, and picked up an adobe brick from a pile beside the house. I pointed at him and grunted, "Hey." Kody's attention turned and he saw the man at the last second, the mud brick lifted over his head. In an instant, Kody grabbed him by his flapping poncho and flung him to the ground.

Immediately, confusingly, cantaloupe-sized boulders rained down from above and crashed into the ground around us. With a sound like thunder they hit the truck, punching the blue sheet metal and thumping the glass over and over, shaking the still night in a symphony of attack, one pop after another, hammering the Toyota along the driver's side and across its hood. The stones bounced and rolled on the ground around us. The dogs growled and tugged all the harder at my pant legs as I stumbled toward the pickup, dragging them along.

At some point the Toyota's back glass exploded. I noticed boulders scattered in the truck bed as I jerked open the door.

Kody looked around. He was as dazed as I was.

"Come on!" I urged, but he was frozen above the fallen Peruvian, his face wrinkled with ire.

Ignorance of the fullness of circumstance had caused us to stop. We stopped as if we were in some leafy American suburb where a soccer mom might grab Junior by the collar of his polo shirt and make him mow our lawns to work off the repairs to the Toyota. Instead, we were in the Wild West. It was after midnight, an hour from the nearest electricity and the nearest police post, our pickup slid to a crooked halt on a gravel road high in the Andes. This was a spot on the globe where less than a decade had passed since Maoist rebels roamed the countryside killing preachers and forcing farmers into their rebel armies. The situation was more dangerous than we appreciated.

Because we were ignorant.

I shook the dogs off my ankles and climbed into the truck.

Kody was as angry as I've ever seen a missionary.

"Come on!" I yelled again, this time from inside the Toyota, over the intermittent thunder of the stones. Kody was having considerably more trouble than I had with the notion of retreat.

Finally, after some final words, he picked his way through the still-flying bombs and dove into the truck.

Before Kody could get the shifter into drive, a stone the size of a potato flew through the busted back window and hit him in the back of the head. He reached a hand to the spot and brought it down covered in blood. He grunted something unintelligible and stepped on the gas pedal.

When we got to the city, Kody drove straight to the police station. It was 2 in the morning, and the outpost was lonely. Dried blood was caked on his neck and matted his blonde hair. He needed stitches, but he wanted justice first.

"We'll go tomorrow," the policeman said. "We aren't going up there tonight. Too dangerous."

The policeman wasn't ignorant.

I was disappointed that I didn't get to make the trip back to Chinchin Tres Cruces the next day with the police. Kody told me later that the homeowner explained the attack by saying a cow thief had stopped the night before we did. While everyone slept, he had stolen a cow. Unbeknownst to us, the night we stopped the whole town had been awake and armed with an arsenal of stones at the ready, hiding in the cornfield above the road and hoping the thief would strike again.

The police told the subsistence farmer he would have to pay restitution for damage to the truck or else the International Mission Board would get his house.

I look back on my 2 years in Peru with a conflicted heart. I helped missionaries meet many people's immediate needs. I don't think they did it in a transactional sort of way, as in, "I'll give you a protein supplement for your malnourished baby if you'll convert to my religion." The medical missions and shoe giveaways and water well projects were always conducted unconditionally. We told them who we worked for, but I don't remember any kind of *quid pro quo*.

But when we weren't doing projects that helped people's physical needs, we were doing outreach. We were salespeople, and I grew to loathe the imposition of my upbringing and culture on people who honestly were smart enough and worldly enough to work out their own salvation, based on their own experiences, true to their own authentic reality. My personal religion was all tangled up with *Hee Haw* and *The Andy Griffith Show* and the summer fun of Vacation Bible School and all these other rural Texas touchstones— which I still love and appreciate—but which honestly had no bearing on the internal dynamics of the typical Peruvian.

Maybe I went native. I stopped seeing myself as the foreigner bringing wisdom and enlightenment with me from my superior shores, my superior upbringing, my superior truth, and I started seeing myself as a 20-something-year-old kid surrounded by other 20-something-year-old kids who just happened to grow up in a different place. The truth is, I probably became a better missionary when I stopped trying to force my barbecued version of my religion on people and started merely relating to them.

We were in this together, me and these other kids. I wasn't there to shine a light for the ignorant masses. We were there together, all of us, to live in community, to get to know one another, to enjoy life and find eternal truths together.

Gradually, I embraced community and rejected values imposition.

Not surprisingly, I didn't win a lot of souls that way. In fact, maybe I lost my own, because my faith grew more nuanced than the know-it-all fundamentalist I had once been would have ever been comfortable with.

When I look at the changes being externally forced on career educators in the United States today by idealistic, privileged

20-somethings, I can't help but think back to those days when I was out insisting on changes, imposing my values—values that aligned with a standards document called *The Baptist Faith and Message*—on people who honestly knew what they were doing without the input of a snotty-nosed entitled American brat, a young person who if he were honest would have admitted he didn't have a clue what he wanted to do with his own life and had little business telling other people what to do with theirs.

I was a well-meaning ignoramus.

✪ SIX ✪

The Educational Dark Ages II: Mendacity

NOT ALL THE MEN WHO TRAVELED to the New World from Europe during the age of exploration came with benign motivations to help the natives find enlightenment or salvation. Some traveled to find rumored lost cities of gold; others looked for the fountain of youth.

That's not to say that they weren't true believers in the faith of the kings and queens that sent them. The conquistadors all claimed the mantle of religion, and proselytizing in large part justified the financing of their missions. But a great many traveled with the first goal of garnering riches and fame for themselves and their patrons; bringing the light of God to the natives was a secondary goal. And more than a few were willing to do nasty things to get the gold they came for.

One such man was the Spanish conquistador Francisco Pizarro.

The Ransom Room

Cajamarca, Peru—my home for 2 years—is home to a large number of intriguing historical sites dating back many centuries. One of the most fascinating is the *Cuarto del Rescate*. It's not much to see: a simple rectangular stone building, relatively small, with little in the way of adornment inside or out. Its name means "ransom room."

According to the Guinness World Records website, the greatest ransom ever paid for the release of a hostage happened in this humble room, back in the 1530s ("Greatest Historical," n.d.). The way my Peruvian friends tell the story, Pizarro and a small band of soldiers had made their way into the land of the Inca. Their timing couldn't have been better: The two sons of the previous Inca ruler, now deceased, had been fighting for power, and the kingdom was split. One of the half-brothers claiming the throne had only recently died in battle, leaving Atahualpa as the *Sapa Inca*, the most-high emperor. Pizarro and his men made contact with Incas loyal to Atahualpa, and they made arrangements to meet him. On the arranged date, thousands of Inca warriors armed with slings and stones accompanied their ruler as he was carried on a litter to meet the tiny band of strangers.

When the Inca emperor drew near, Pizarro unleashed an audacious and treacherous plan. Armed with swords, and with artillery and cavalry hidden in nearby buildings, Pizarro's men charged the king and fought off his army of lightly armed defenders, killing a large number. They captured Atahualpa and the Incas retreated.

Pizarro had Atahualpa—the emperor of the largest, most advanced civilization in South America—locked in a tiny room, and he began negotiations with him and his followers.

When I visited the *Cuarto del Rescate*, I noticed a faint red line painted on the interior wall, about seven or eight feet off the floor, going all the way around the room. According to the story, in an effort to save his life and upon learning that the Spaniards loved gold and silver, Atahualpa reached his hand up as high as he could and pledged to have his people fill the room with gold and silver.

Pizarro agreed, and the Incas began turning their riches over to the brash intruders. According to my wife's version of the history, the Incas filled the room twice with silver and once with gold. Guinness World Records says the ransom paid for Atahualpa was worth over $1 billion in today's money ("Greatest Historical," n.d.).

In the end, Pizarro got his gold and on August 29, 1533, in one of history's most offensive acts of deceitfulness, he executed Atahualpa anyway. Pizarro ordered that a trial be held and the Inca king was found guilty of revolt against the Spanish, idolatry, and killing his half-brother Huascar. Others who would futilely rebel against the encroaching Spanish dominance would later claim the title of *Sapa Inca*, but Atahualpa was the last of the true Inca kings.

Pizarro perhaps believed the gospel of the priests who accompanied him in his travels, but in the end he was a man of action, not principles. In a similar vein, school reform investors and think tank mouthpieces may parrot the heartfelt exuberance for mission expressed by passionate Teach for America true believers, but their motivations are undoubtedly rarely as noble or selfless as the calling to save America's desperately neglected youth that inspires white hat reformers like Jessica Reid.

Disruptive Heroes and Status Quo Villains: The Lies of Reform

Steve Brill, the aforementioned author of *Class Warfare*, speaks a lot about heroes and villains in his writing about education, and he does so with a striking uniformity of classification. No-excuses charter school champions are invariably heroes in the tales Brill tells, and union-stifled traditional school employees are generally villains.

An objective study of the historical record reveals that Brill's implied dichotomy is a carefully curated construct with little relation to reality. In truth, there are heroes and villains on both sides of the reform divide. There are certainly incompetent teachers and disengaged administrators—villains—scattered among our traditional schools, but they work alongside any number of heroic, selfless, dedicated colleagues who teach ably and determinedly for all the right reasons. Likewise, the world of no-excuses schools isn't solely inhabited by martyrs and strong-chinned champions, despite the fact that raconteurs like Brill and friends tend to employ hyper-valiant terms like "Superman" and "miracle school."

I once listened as a high school principal who had written provocative books about school reform described the miraculous results he had gotten in his inner-city school. He noted that 100% of his students graduated each year and went on to a 4-year college. Not a crummy community college, mind you; a 4-year college.

These were inner-city kids, as poor as they come, and he was getting them into universities. All of them.

As if to preemptively silence the cynics, he informed us that he didn't run a charter school. He looked us all in the eye. He ran a public high school, emphasis on the word "public," thank you very much.

I condemned myself privately as the man spoke. The teachers in the audience probably joined me. We were the problem with the American education system, and the man before us was the solution.

The reformer had found the elixir sought since at least 1983. He had the answer to our failing schools crisis in the palm of his hand, and he was kind enough to share it with us. The rest of us were lost souls in need of his tutelage; we didn't even realize how lazy and pathetic we were, how useless our daily efforts were. It was sad, really, how lost and foolish we were.

I wish I had checked his claims out on my smart phone as I sat there. I should have. The thought ran through my mind as he spoke: What if this guy is lying? Why am I beating myself up when his big talk is completely unverified?

But he had a best-selling book. Surely no one is audacious enough to build a career based on misinformation. Or so I thought.

After the conference, hoping to find confirmation that I wasn't as bad as he made me feel, I checked this fellow's school website and promptly discovered what I and all the browbeaten teachers present must have suspected: His public school didn't take all comers as ours did. The principal oversaw a magnet school. He only took kids who qualified. Yes, they were poor, but they weren't apathetic. They were filtered through a fine mesh of minimum-score requirements and parental obligations. This wasn't a school you could fairly compare to regular traditional public schools with no enrollment restrictions. That didn't keep him from doing just that, however. And he did so without disclosing exactly what kind of school his was.

He lied. It was by omission rather than commission, but it was still a lie, nothing more and nothing less. He tricked me and a roomful of college professors and browbeaten K–12 teachers into thinking he was better than us at our lives' missions.

This man's calculating deceitfulness ruined me on school reform, not that I was particularly convinced of its claims beforehand. I determined, as I sat staring at my computer screen and muttering unkind words, that self-promoters and phonies owned the movement. I concluded that my state's leaders and, in fact, leaders nationwide were being led astray by duplicitous hucksters.

I decided to match the story this guy peddled with my own, and to tell it from the mountains. While he said children were the victims of bad teachers, I would contend that children were the victims of bad policy. I would drown out his mean-spirited, self-serving song about teachers who shatter children with my own praises for teachers who find children already broken and struggle amid a cacophony of recriminations to repair them.

"Government Schools"

"Schools are failing" is a persistent and useful meme. The ball really got rolling with the publication of *A Nation at Risk* in 1983. That singular publication and the decades-long onslaught of crisis journalism spawned by it miraculously tied conservatives who were chiefly concerned about the growth of government and taxation to liberals who agonized over the plight of poor and minority youth. The right and the left were able to stop firing their guns at one another for a while and could both focus their aim on the teachers in our public schools.

The dramatic emergence of Ron Paul–style libertarian populism and the Tea Party movement in and around 2010 gave the "schools are failing" meme new vigor. Anything run by government was automatically inefficient and monopolistic. No data was even needed to establish it; this indisputable fact was self-evident. Suddenly, it did no good for teachers or public education supporters—"defenders of the status quo"—to produce data indicating that American students were improving or that performance gaps between subpopulations were narrowing. Data could do nothing to defeat a blind faith in the absolute superiority of the free market. Public schools weren't bad because the data suggested it anymore; they were bad because they were *public.*

The shift from a bipartisan data-driven angst about American students' performance on international tests to a more partisan faith-based conviction that public schools were intrinsically beyond redemption (and couldn't improve even if they wanted to) is evident in the language used in the debate. The derisive phrase "government schools" replaced "public schools" (with its inconvenient positive historical connotations) among the most ardent foes of public expenditure and taxation.

Teachers were like the stunned attendants of Atahualpa as wild-eyed true believers essentially yelled "Charge!" on their Internet forums, proclaiming that teachers, by virtue of their getting a paycheck funded with state and local revenues, were sworn enemies of liberty.

It's disconcerting to wake up one day and realize that you're the accidental enemy of zealous ideologues, and to know you attained this status merely by virtue of living what you thought was a modest life. There's a peculiar heartbreak that attends the discovery that you're despised after spending a quiet lifetime anonymously engaging in what you had thought was a modest, benign, even helpful, and patriotic service-oriented profession.

A Warning from the Blueberry Man

Jamie Vollmer is a hero to the teachers who learn about him. Photocopies of his "Blueberry Story" are hung up like religious icons in who knows how many teachers' lounges around the country. His story gives teachers hope. It is the story of a highly successful businessman who, like many prominent businessmen today, took an interest in education and came to the field with a generally negative view of the work being done by teachers in public schools.

I had the privilege of hearing Vollmer recount this story to a group of Texas superintendents in early 2013.

Vollmer's "Blueberry Story" tells of an incident that happened when he spoke to a group of teachers about excellence and innovation, topics which he at the time was sure those teachers needed to hear more about. In his speech, he told the teachers his own personal history. Vollmer had started an ice cream company and his ice cream had felicitously been named "the best ice cream in the country" by a number of prominent national magazines. Who better to bring a message of excellence to our substandard public teaching corps?

Vollmer told the crowd that his success was a direct result of his high standards—he only put out the very best product possible. That was his secret. He didn't skimp on the cream. He only used the best blueberries he could get.

Then, as Vollmer tells it, an older teacher in the back of the room slipped her hand in the air.

"What do you do if you get a bad shipment of blueberries?" she asked.

"I send them back," he answered cavalierly.

He said he didn't hear the trap snap until it was too late.

"We don't get to do that," she said. "We get bad blueberries too, but we have to teach them."

Vollmer told us that was his epiphany, and since then he has traveled the nation telling teachers to heed the advice of Abraham Lincoln: You can't win if public opinion is against you, and you can't lose if it's with you.

Public education supporters, Vollmer has argued, have badly lost the public relations war by complacently assuming the nation loved teachers and always would. Teachers and their supporters neglected to tell their stories and counter the influence of those whose ideology requires them to tear down public schools and, collaterally, the people who work in them.

After receiving an award for his tireless advocacy, Vollmer issued a warning to those who care about public schools:

> Public education is under attack as never before. Bashing public schools has become a blood sport—a dangerous game in which sensational headlines publicize half-truths, statistics are used out of context, and test results are reported in the worst possible light. (Friends of Texas Public Schools, 2012)

The opposition to public education is so strident and, from the perspective of teachers, mean-spirited, that teachers aren't sure what to do to restore themselves to a place of dignity in the sight of the nation. Fear initiated by *A Nation at Risk* aligned liberals and conservatives in a campaign to "fix" public education, but it went off the rails. Today, self-proclaimed liberals like Michelle Rhee and Arne Duncan find themselves allied with any number of free market absolutists because the enemy of bad teachers is their friend.

Sadly, the campaign to fix public schools is being (or has been) hijacked by a campaign to end them. And that campaign isn't interested in truth or right conclusions or the honest use of data. It is wholly devoted to the installation of a free market educational system, absolutely convinced that—despite many decades of American excellence with a public school system serving the vast majority of the children—there is no other way to successfully educate children. School reformers who tell half-truths to advance their careers or boost their number of TV appearances are useful to this mission. Compassionate true believers who are properly appalled by the conditions faced by children in underfunded public schools are also useful to this mission. Data—which can be twisted and spun any which way—is especially useful to this mission.

A few Milton Friedman acolytes truly want to "privatize education." But a very large number of well-meaning dupes are helping them do it.

The Reign of Deceit

When a Socratic pursuit of truth stops being the point of a debate and it becomes clear that an untruthful rhetorician wants a win any way he or she can get it, the honest arguer has no choice but to conclude that arguing is fruitless. The other person's mind is made up, and specious means—skewed statistics, anecdotes and outliers presented as evidence, dubious research—are hard to confront.

A mendacious person doesn't engage in mendacity for no reason, nor usually just for the thrill of telling a fib. Mendacious reasoning is deployed to win arguments and, oftentimes, to sell ideas that may not work as advertised.

When it comes to education in Texas, the bandying forth of self-proclaimed experts who lack any real objective proof of their expertise is an old game. In setting history standards, the Texas State Board of Education relied on the testimony of David Barton, a self-proclaimed expert in American history who has devoted his career to proving that the founding fathers never intended for there to be a separation of church and state in America. David Barton is, in simplest terms, a proponent of American theocracy. His writings are imbued with an appearance of scholarship that manages to fool some of the people some of the time. In fact, he was able to fool many of the people in Texas for a long, long time, mainly because he was willing to tell them what they wanted to hear.

Barton's authority took quite a hit with the publication in 2012 of his book *The Jefferson Lies*. Named "the least credible history book in print," *The Jefferson Lies* included, according to critics, what Barton "likes about Jefferson and leaves out the rest to create a result more in line with his ideology" (Schuessler, 2012). Even friendly reviewers questioned the accuracy of the book's claims, and Thomas Nelson, the Christian publishing company that produced the book, incredibly chose to withdraw it from publication—that is, to take the almost-unprecedented step of pulling an already-printed book from the shelves and to simply eat the cost of printing—because they had "lost confidence in the book's details" (Kidd, 2012).

Climate scientists dealing with similarly mendacious opponents have been loath to overstep "perceived boundaries of prudence, objectivity, and statistical error bars" and directly confront the disingenuous argumentation facing them (Mingle, 2012). Nevertheless, the existential danger many climate scientists foresee if their science isn't trusted has prompted some to overcome professional or personal reservations about speaking out. Some have been arrested at environmental protests. One jolted the scientific community by giving a presentation called "Is Earth F**ked?" at a conference (Mingle, 2012).

The geophysicist behind the profanely named presentation explained that he adopted the shocking title in response to the fact that there is "good science . . . being done all over the world," yet the world has a "seeming inability to respond appropriately to it" (Mingle, 2012).

Speaking out about destructive education policies is likewise fraught with complications and career-compromising threats. Particularly in today's highly partisan environment, opposing the Republican Party's plans for education in a place like Texas or the Democratic Party's plans for education in a place like Washington, DC, can lead to serious doubts locally about one's fitness to educate that community's children.

After I spoke at the 2011 Save Texas Schools rally, a gentleman sent my school board president a letter complaining that I was associating with socialists. One person on the guiding committee of the organization that sponsored the rally—a person I had never heard of nor met—was apparently affiliated with a teacher's union in Houston. This was enough for one person to question my American credentials.

The smear hurt me almost physically. I consider myself a proud citizen who cares deeply for the future of our society. My patriotism and love for my state and country, in fact, were key reasons why I chose to speak at the rally.

Like scientists who see threats posed to the planet by climate change, I sincerely believe that the utter demolition of public education is eventual, perhaps even imminent, under today's reform banner, and that despite their imperfections public schools are our nation's most democratizing structure. My outspokenness may have guaranteed that some school districts will never hire me: Who wants to hire a troublemaker? But if my silence would give aid to those whose goals are antithetical to my own dreams for my children, what should I do?

The fact is, our grim march toward the end of this fundamental American tradition—a free public education for all children—will only proceed if supporters of public education by their acquiescence allow it.

✪ SEVEN ✪

Why We Don't Fix Things

THE VOLUNTEERS HAD COME FROM an American seminary. There were two guys, brothers, and a handful of girls. They stayed for a month or so painting churches, performing puppet shows, and sharing Bible stories with Andean children who giggled at their blonde locks and their smiling pink mouths. My job was twofold: I was to shepherd them here and there in my 1970-something Toyota pickup, and I was to play host to the two guys in my house while the girls stayed with a female mission worker 15 miles up the road in Baños del Inca.

"The Gringo Did It"

THE NIGHT BEFORE THE VOLUNTEERS were to fly home also happened to be the night of the annual Sugar Cane Festival in Baños del Inca. The Americans took advantage of the opportunity to pick up some last-minute souvenirs and watch beautiful Peruvian Paso horses prancing gingerly and local marinera dancers twirling their traditional red scarves.

It must've been 11 or 12 at night when the guys were ready for me to take them back to my house. One brother climbed into the back seat with an alpaca backpack full of souvenirs; the other slid into the front.

The highway between Baños del Inca and the city of Cajamarca was dark and narrow, a two-lane blacktop cutting through empty fields that reminded me a great deal of the lonelier stretches of Highway 281 back home.

That particular night, we followed two late city buses, each packed with people heading home from the festival. The lights were on inside the buses and I watched the riders. There is something forlorn about people staring out of bus windows at night.

Suddenly, the first bus cut sharply into the oncoming lane, then back again. The next bus did the same thing, just as suddenly, and I watched the heads of the riders in the back seat swivel as they tried to see what their bus had swerved to avoid.

After the second bus dodged, my headlights illuminated the body of a woman sprawled in the middle of the road.

To be perfectly honest, I badly wanted to keep driving, just as the two buses had. But I had a part to play for my two passengers: Missionaries don't drive past accident victims and leave them lying in the middle of the highway.

I pulled into the oncoming lane and stopped beside the woman. I turned on my flashers and took a deep breath.

"Stop traffic coming from that direction," I instructed the brother in the front seat. It sounded reasonable. It came out confidently. "I'll stop traffic in this direction." The façade that I knew what I was doing held for the moment.

"What do I do? What do I do? What do I do?" my mind shouted as I flagged down the cars coming toward us from the west. I hoped a doctor would jump out of one of the cars and come help us.

No doctor came to save me from decisionmaking. With the traffic stopped, there was only one other thing left to do. I had to go see about the woman.

I approached slowly and immediately noticed a black, thick pool of blood on the asphalt behind her head. There were chunks of white tissue in the pool. Her face was pale and swollen. Her eyes were closed.

I glanced up at the stopped traffic coming from Baños del Inca. Headlights stretched for miles. A mustachioed fireplug of a Peruvian came from somewhere and offered to help. I was hoping he would take charge. He didn't.

"We should call 911," said the younger American.

"There's no 911 here," I replied.

Countless headlights were stacked in both directions. There were no other roads but this one between the larger city of Cajamarca and the smaller city where the massive fair had just taken place. I didn't know what to do.

"We've got to get out of the way of all these cars," I told the older brother. The younger brother said he needed to throw up.

Gurgling noises came from the woman. Maybe she was alive? But there were brains on the pavement. She had to be dead. But all those cars? They stretched as far as the eye could see.

I slow-played it. I hoped a cop would show up.

She was an Andean Indian woman, maybe in her 30s. Her skirts—the *campesinas* wore layers of often bright, neon skirts—were thrown up so that you could see her private parts. I wondered if I should cover her up.

I didn't want to move her. I didn't want to touch her. I didn't want to be anywhere near her broken head.

As I wrestled with what to do—scared, young, brash—a man with a scrape on his face walked up out of the darkness from the side of the road. He wore a crimson poncho with cream trim, the style that the Cajamarca *campesinos* all wore. This was the husband.

"*Tenemos que llevarla*," I said. "We have to take her."

The man was worried about his bicycle. They'd been hit as they pedaled down the slender shoulder of the highway in the pitch black night, a night of heavy *cañazo*-drinking for many fair-goers, if not for the stricken husband.

He wanted his bicycle. It was his only transportation. And their shoes had flown off. We needed to find those. There was a bag somewhere too. He wanted us to find those things.

I asked the American brothers to seek and gather the couple's scattered belongings. The younger brother would have to ride in the bed of the pickup so the man and his broken wife could ride in the back seat.

"You get her head," I told the husband. I couldn't find a gentler way to say it. He nodded. He was dazed. I grabbed her feet and fixed her skirts, and we lugged her limp frame into the truck. She was still gurgling. He cradled her shattered head in his lap, lovingly.

I was smart enough to know that you shouldn't move a dead body from the scene of an accident. But all those cars. I half-convinced myself that she might be alive because of the noises. We'd been there with traffic stopped for what seemed like forever. We had to get out of the way. I didn't know what to do.

We moved a dead body from the scene of an accident.

The brothers loaded up all the man's stuff they could find and jumped in. They had found the bike. I floored the Toyota and we sped up my empty lane of the highway.

I didn't know what to say, so I simply asked the man if he was a *creyente*, a believer. He said yes, and I said something that burns my ears 2 decades later with its clumsy sanctimony.

"Pray," I ordered him, as if I was a high priest with full understanding of God and life and death. She was dead. Praying for her wouldn't help. I don't know why I said it; just to have something to say, I guess. It was easier than saying, "Your wife is dead."

A watchman guarding a storefront blew his whistle as I barreled the wrong way up a one-way street near the hospital. The pickup squealed to a halt in the parking lot and the volunteers and I jumped out. I ran in to the emergency room and told the lady at the reception desk that I had a badly injured woman in my vehicle. I needed a doctor.

A doctor and the husband placed the shattered woman onto a gurney and wheeled her into the hospital while we Americans unloaded the couple's belongings. I found a police officer at a guard shack and asked if I needed to give a statement. I asked if he wanted to make a copy of my driver's license. He said no, but thanks for bringing her in.

The next morning, the older brother and I wiped blood from the vinyl back seat of my pickup.

We took the group out to lunch just before their flight was to leave Cajamarca, to this little restaurant where you could eat in a courtyard surrounded by monkeys chained to trees, listening to toucans squawk in birdcages. The meal was good.

Just before we left, one of the brothers looked up.

"My backpack," he exclaimed. "I bought an alpaca backpack at the festival. It was full of souvenirs for my family. Someone must have accidentally unloaded it at the hospital."

When I pulled into the hospital parking lot, the backpack became less important. There were police cars there, more than I expected to see. I went inside and told the lady at the emergency reception desk about the backpack. She had it under the counter.

She gave it to me, and when I turned around, a number of police officers were looking at me. One of them asked me if I was the guy who had brought in the lady the night before. She had been dead on arrival, he said. I would need to go to the *municipalidad* and give a statement.

I called my boss and let him know I was going to the police station. He was at the airport with the volunteers, but he would join me soon.

The interview started at 1 or 2 in the afternoon. A grandfatherly police officer asked me questions and typed my answers painstakingly on a clattering manual typewriter. The interview lasted for hours; most of the time either Kody or a local pastor was there helping to translate my imperfect Spanish.

I would be there until midnight.

They came in at some point and took my keys. The truck was impounded. They needed to see if it had any signs of having hit the couple on the bicycle. They would look for dents, blood, hair, and tissues.

Dents? It was a 1970s-era Toyota pickup that had been used in the mission field in Peru for decades. It had more dents than smooth spots.

The husband showed up at the police station after a few hours. I nodded a greeting, and he nodded back. They led him to the room next door. I assumed he was answering their questions too.

A stream of visitors came to see the husband. One old man in a poncho told the young widower that I probably worked for *la mina*. Yanacocha, the largest gold mine in the world, was just outside of town. Most of the gringos in that part of the world weren't missionaries; they were either European backpackers or engineers and executives for the Canadian mining company.

The way I interpreted it, what the old man really meant was that I probably had money.

Then I heard him say, "The gringo did it. His truck is red, and there's red paint on the bicycle."

Red paint? I got scared.

During a break, I went to the courtyard where the mangled bicycle leaned against a wall. The back wheel was caved in. I looked it over for red paint, expecting to see streaks of red against the crumpled back end. The only paint I saw—to my relief—was in the form of several tiny drips where someone had painted something above the bike and the paint had spattered down, leaving tear-shaped speckles. They weren't even the right shade of red. But the words rang in my head: "The gringo did it."

I had heard tales of police officers taking bribes. My mind ran away with the paranoid thought. What if the police officer examining my truck needed money? What if he thought that I made a boatload working for the gold mine, and what if he decided to tell me it would take $10,000 for him to release my truck and declare me innocent?

I didn't have $10,000, and I was willing to bet that my parents didn't either. Maybe they could get a loan. The mission board had required me to sign an affidavit affirming my understanding of its policy not to pay bribes or ransoms.

I knew an honest examination of my truck would conclude I was innocent, but if this was a crooked cop, I was in trouble.

After I had been at the police station for a very long time, the old cop who had excruciatingly typed my statement came in and smiled kindly.

"They're finished with your vehicle," he said. "The bicycle was hit low to the ground by a small car. Your pickup is too high to have done it."

He handed me the keys and thanked me for stopping to help. Case closed. Kody slapped a hand on my back and I exhaled.

"Can you do me a favor?" the police officer asked as we gathered our things.

Sure, man. Anything.

The husband was still in the next room and all his family had gone. The buses had stopped for the night. He had no way home—his bike was trashed.

"Could you give him a ride?"

I was sure this man was convinced I had killed his wife. I'd heard his visitors arguing my guilt. I somewhat randomly convinced myself that he probably had a screwdriver under his poncho and would love to drive it through my skull.

"Sure, I'll give him a ride," I said.

Kody lived in Baños del Inca, and the man's village of Tar Tar was up in the dark and lonely mountains a good ways past there. I wanted to ask Kody if he would stay in the car and ride with me all the way to Tar Tar on account of my irrational screwdriver fears, but I couldn't figure out how to ask. If I spoke in English, the grieving husband might think I was confessing something nefarious to my American co-conspirator. And I couldn't very well come out and say, in Spanish, "Hey Kody, I'm scared this guy sitting behind us may kill me if you leave me alone with him." I didn't want to give him any ideas.

So I dropped Kody off at his house and I drove up into the remote mountains with a grieving husband sitting directly behind me in the darkness. I couldn't stop thinking about the screwdriver. I tried hard to be discreet when I adjusted my rearview mirror so I could see him.

"Turn here," he said. I turned off the highway onto a gravel road. We drove for ages.

"Are we getting close?" I kept asking. "Are we almost there?"

The next turn was onto a road of sandy dirt and, several long minutes later, we turned onto a grassy trail cut through a pasture. We were far away from everything, in a place I had never been.

We finally crested a low rise and I saw two adobe houses in the distance, with lanterns reflecting off their windows. A crowd of what had to be hundreds surrounded the nearest one, the scene glinting with dozens of torches and a rolling bonfire.

"*Vivo en la segunda casa,*" he told me. He lived in the second house.

The crowd and the torches were 50 yards away. I slowed to a stop beside a lonely black tree in the pasture. I assumed they were mourning his wife. I assumed they were drinking *cañazo*. I assumed they were angry.

I apologized to my passenger. "I'm sorry, but this is as far as I go."

The man thanked me and climbed out of the truck. After he was clear, I jerked it into reverse and bounced through the pasture in the opposite direction as fast as I could, half-convinced I would get lost before I made it back to an actual road.

I thought about something the kind officer said to me before I had left the police station that night, as he apologized for my inconvenience.

"This is why," he told me, "no one in this town stops to help."

The buses that night didn't stop to render aid for one reason: the cost might've been too high.

A Man, a Plan

Progress on any front is often slowed or prevented less by an inability to overcome a given problem and more by the shaky will of those who resist intervention. Many dig in because they fret over the size of the called-for investment; others don't like the intrusion of a new science or technology on their personal dogmata or cherished traditions.

In the rhetoric that accompanies today's changes in how we do schooling, those on the side of reform often acknowledge this reality and paint teachers as the fearful status quo, holding back a positive revolution. From many teachers' perspective, however, it is the multimillionaire businessperson intent on expanding the scope of the market who represents a dogged and destructive orthodoxy. Converting America's educational commons into a bustling commercial sector isn't really revolutionary at all. We have seen this neoliberal movie over and over, especially since our government landed contentedly on the short leash of campaign donors.

In today's shifting educational landscape, the expanding opportunities for major-league investors dwarf the supposedly expanding opportunities for children. The clearest beneficiaries of many of today's canonical education reforms are not the children, but hedge funders and CEOs. Outside of the anecdotes they cling to, in fact, there is little to show, statistically speaking, for the massive upheavals education reform has thrust on America's schools. Decades of punitive coercion and privatization have resulted in only one indisputably rising graph line: the one representing the value of edu-investor portfolios.

The leaders of a real revolution on behalf of struggling Americans wouldn't be marketing touchscreen tablets to schoolchildren. They wouldn't be fighting to co-locate their privately run schools in buildings paid for by taxpayers, shouldering out the common school brats along the way. They wouldn't pitch online courses taught by overstretched (and, sometimes, inadequately certified) teachers as some sort of felicitously profitable panacea. They wouldn't charge struggling school districts millions in fees for the privilege of placing their corps of enthusiastic 2-year interns in classrooms. They wouldn't work overtime to align national Common Core State Standards to an SAT test their firm happens to own the exclusive rights to. These are not the movements of rabble-rousers or insurgents; this is the establishment hard at work maintaining the status quo.

A truly revolutionary billionaire would insist that school funding be equitably spent and that taxation to fund schools be adequate to the task of providing a quality education in every neighborhood, for all American kids, and not just lottery winners. The real insurrection would be if Americans of wealth and political clout were to take a hard look at nations that outperform America, not only on international academic tests but also on statistics relating to child poverty levels, and then sought to implement strategies to improve the whole condition of the child, not just their aggregate test scores.

Real solutions to real problems exist, and their cost is normally commensurate with the damage they attempt to undo. Meanwhile, pseudosolutions are comparatively cheap and easy; they offer the balm of just "doing something," without the unpopular downside of requiring an investment equal to the challenge.

Education reform as it has been popularly implemented since George W. Bush introduced No Child Left Behind is an example of the latter. Expensive correctives like school funding equity and wraparound social services for children who lack basic things that middle- and upper-class Americans take for granted have taken a back seat to cheaper alternatives. The administration of mass-produced bubble tests is cheaper than an equal educational investment in Americans of all stripes, as are reductions in funding for schools where students don't do well on those tests.

We are perhaps supposed to believe it is a coincidence that virtually all of today's bipartisan education solutions—from the elimination of due process in teacher firings, to the closing of neighborhood schools and the emergence of for-profit charter chains, to virtual education, to school vouchers—either reduce the taxation needed to fund schooling or else increase the proportion of education spending funneled toward private sector players. Reflecting on the impact of the Common Core State Standards movement, Arne Duncan's chief of staff Joanne Weiss wrote plainly in *Harvard Business Review* that "the adoption of common standards and shared assessments means that education entrepreneurs will enjoy national markets" (Weiss, 2011). About the children, indeed. News Corp.'s Rupert Murdoch added his two cents when he famously noted that the American education sector is a $500 billion market "waiting desperately to be transformed" by for-profit interests (Kamenetz, 2013).

In short, the private sector will either spend less on education or else make more off of it, or, preferably, both. Today's education reforms have this in common: They drive dollars from the public school system and into the waiting hands of the business class, and as private coffers swell, America watches massive public school systems from Detroit to Philadelphia collapse under fiscal strain.

These reforms are presented to the public as being "about the children." But, as one journalist noted, it "strains credulity to insist that pedagogues who get paid middling wages but nonetheless devote their lives to educating kids care less about those kids than do the Wall Street hedge funders and billionaire CEOs who finance the so-called reform movement" (Sirota, 2013).

Digging the Panama Canal was a difficult task. The French had tried and failed. Theodore Roosevelt was determined to complete it, and he did. One of the problems that hampered construction was a staggering death toll among workers from diseases like yellow fever. After Dr. Walter Reed confirmed that mosquitoes served as vectors for many tropical diseases, the Roosevelt administration implemented a massive—and massively expensive—sanitation and mosquito abatement program in the Canal Zone. It involved paving roads to eliminate standing water, isolating sick workers, installing proper screens on worker housing, and using pesticides and burning sulfur to kill mosquitoes. The project, which largely eradicated the deadly diseases in the Canal Zone, was described as an example of "what medical science can accomplish when properly backed by government" (Bennett, 1915).

Despite what many pundits and talking heads adamantly preach, dramatic and life-enhancing progress is possible at the intersection of confident knowledge and sufficient resources. Theodore Roosevelt knew that, and he didn't let cheapskates and misers—mad that their tax contributions were being squandered in Central America, mad that Roosevelt was "throwing money at the problem," to borrow today's never-spend rhetoric—slow down progress.

Mesquite Trees

MESQUITE TREES ARE AN invasive species; they offer a perfect metaphor for the folly of substituting fake solutions for real, albeit costlier, ones. Mesquite trees are great for barbecuing but terrible for everything else. There are two ways to get rid of them. The cheap and easy way—cut them down—doesn't really work. It appears to work, because the mesquite tree is gone, but mesquite trees have a long tap root that plunges deep through dry Texas soil until it finds water. When the tree is cut down, the root doesn't die; the tree comes back, as hardy and thorny as ever. To get rid of a mesquite tree, you have to grub it up by the roots. This requires equipment, ideally a trackhoe (a backhoe on tracks instead of tires).

A chainsaw is much cheaper, of course, and it can make it look like you've cleared a field of mesquite trees, but it takes something bigger to actually get the job done.

You can remove mesquite trees on the cheap. Or you can really remove mesquite trees.

The Well-Meaning
and the Self-Serving, Allied

Convinced that poverty and broad, unfettered inequity are too big of nuts to crack in America, liberal school reformers have turned their attention to much cheaper schemes for rescuing the oppressed, like mass-produced and mass-graded tests, scripted teaching techniques, virtual schools and other "disruptive technologies," low-experience interns, and deregulated schools called charters. All of these approaches demonstrate real promise for lowering the property tax rates of corporations and individuals of high wealth; few if any show definitive benefits for children's learning, but no matter. School reformers are convinced that anything at all is better than what we've done since the beginning. The move toward these low-cost fixes was accelerated when investors and CEOs with stakes in educational technology or charter school management organizations joined the chorus of the true believers.

This alliance of the well-meaning and the self-serving pushes for an education policy menu that boils down to a timid avoidance of the daunting root causes of our nation's educational malaise.

It is ultimately cheaper and faster to cut down unions than it is to dig up our structural inequalities. And so, the reformers who present themselves as far more compassionate than the people who teach our children are strangely silent when it comes to the widely known practice of inequitably funding our children's education. That particular injustice is ignored in the reform playbook.

Sputnik Moments

On October 4, 1957, the USSR launched a manmade satellite named Sputnik into orbit around the Earth. The average American reacted in shock at the news and the nation was stirred to suddenly and dramatically increase military spending and public investments in math and science education.

Sputnik has been fixed in the American mind ever since. It is an object lesson about what happens when we get complacent as a people, when we let other nations slip ahead of us in what we think is a zero-sum race to cultural and economic greatness.

Anything can be a Sputnik moment now.

In his 2011 State of the Union address, President Obama referred to the sharp disappointment and near-panic that seized our nation after the satellite's launch. "This is our Sputnik moment," he intoned gravely, referring to the fiscal, social, and educational challenges that faced us in those days. He called on the American people to join with him in an effort to "win the future" (Kornblut & Wilson, 2011).

But the night of that State of the Union address wasn't truly "a Sputnik moment." Even a gifted orator like our 44th president couldn't craft such a crisis out of mere words.

You need a satellite for a "Sputnik moment." Barring that, you need some other actual, physical, tangible manifestation of American defeat. The American people need to see a black eye in the mirror before they will fully accept the notion that they've lost a fight.

We got a pretty good shiner months later. Of all days, the whipping happened on Independence Day in 2012. Scientists at Europe's Large Hadron Collider (LHC) announced they had all but discovered the Higgs boson, a tiny particle that sticks to all other particles like syrup and gives them mass. No one knows yet how this discovery will ultimately impact human life, but past discoveries on the subatomic level have led to paradigm-shattering innovations in medicine, communications, electronics, computing, and other fields. They have opened up whole new industries that humankind never would have envisioned absent the discoveries. In fact, the most significant of the LHC's contributions to humankind happened long before it discovered anything: international scientists sharing data from the LHC had created "the internet's World Wide Web, which was invented . . . to aid communication between particle physicists across the globe" (Von Radowitz, 2012).

The Higgs discovery will undoubtedly lead to similarly valuable advances which will benefit people around the globe. The United States of America should have discovered it. In fact, the United States should have discovered the Higgs boson about 10 years sooner than the Europeans.

In 1983, the United States proposed an ambitious project along the lines of the LHC. Construction began in 1991, giving America a decade's head start on the Europeans. The program was called the Superconducting Supercollider, and it was to be built just outside of Dallas, Texas. It was planned to be larger than the LHC and would have smashed particles together with three times the energy. Not only would we have had a head start on the quest for the legendary particle, but our progress toward the Higgs would have likely been faster because of the greater size and power of the Superconducting Supercollider.

After investing $2 billion in the project, however, American elected officials got cold feet. They wavered; they didn't like spending all that money. Ultimately, lacking the gumption of a Theodore Roosevelt, our leaders walked away from the dollar cost of progress. They shuttered the giant hole in the ground outside of Dallas and left the Higgs boson for the Europeans to find.

In terms of American audacity, it was the equivalent of stopping work on Mount Rushmore somewhere between Thomas Jefferson's nose and his mouth.

"I couldn't believe it," said Nobel Prize–winning physicist Steven Weinberg (Gioja & O'Connor, 2012). The nation's scientists were stunned and disheartened.

The day of reckoning for this decision came on July 4, 2012, a click on America's timeline more like the original Sputnik than any other claimed Sputnik moment before or since.

It shouldn't surprise us that American leaders in the 1990s shuttered an expensive project with esoteric scientific aims. It's hard to convince our politicians to fund things they can't understand. Furthermore, fiscal conservatism is the coin of the realm now, and it was then as well. Politicians lap up statements from think tanks, and when the Heritage Foundation says "There is nothing that government can do that we cannot do better as free individuals" and "Without big government, our possibilities our limitless," our leaders appear to believe them (Heritage Foundation, 2012). Perhaps they don't know about the inspiring persistence and massive investment Theodore Roosevelt's government provided—*successfully*—to give the world the Panama Canal.

Nothing government can do that we can't do better as individuals? I'm no expert, but it appears to me that government is better than individuals at building canals and finding bosons. The Higgs boson, in fact, seems to reside contentedly somewhere beyond the purportedly limitless bounds of individual freedom. It wasn't a group of rugged individualists who brought the LHC to life and found Higgs, after all; it was a coalition of European social democracies.

And now, the Europeans are standing at the forefront of science and discovery, and we Americans are the proud owners of a big hole in the ground.

But, hey, at least we saved the money we would have spent on the Superconducting Supercollider, right? Wrong. We spent what would have been the full cost of the particle smasher on war-fighting in Iraq many, many times over.

In the end, the politicians who shuttered the American particle smasher were never really fiscally conservative. They were something more along the lines of fiscal redirectors. Throughout the modern history of the republic, self-proclaimed frugal leaders have cried fiscal calamity each time science or education or public health or any other public good came calling, only to forget austerity ever existed when generals needed a whiz bang or big business needed a tax break. It isn't that "limited government" never loosens its purse strings; that's a falsehood. Limited government spends quite remarkably; it's just that it asks regular people to make way for special citizens who qualify for business class democracy when it does.

The original Sputnik moment spurred a reevaluation of our educational system and our military preparedness. The 2012 Higgs moment should cause us to reconsider a prevailing American values system that demands ever less investment in our collective good so that we can spend more on the good of a tiny pool of big money (and big influence) citizens. This kind of leadership leaves us watching the Higgs boson slip out of our hand and into the grasp (thankfully) of our allies.

Next time we might not be so lucky.

The Steamroller

A popular phrase in modern educational discourse is "the achievement gap."

Dr. Camika Royal was a former Teach for America intern who became a darling of the pro-public education movement after video surfaced of her speaking at a summer TFA institute in Philadelphia and bluntly challenging the anti-teacher, us-versus-them rhetoric that had become popular and predictable among education reformers. In late 2012, she made waves again by challenging the use of the term "achievement gap" as a racist construct. She did so first in a post on the Philadelphia Public School Notebook blog, and then she elaborated on her point of view in a November guest post at Diane Ravitch's blog.

Dr. Royal summarized her problem with "achievement gap" thinking:

> What extends from the notion of the "achievement gap" is a messiah complex that fuels people rallied around "saving" children from themselves, their families, and their communities. Education reformers' messiah complex manifests in the belief that the end (a "shot" in life via high test scores) justifies the means (mechanized and routinized instruction, ignoring or dismissing community input and cultural contexts, steamrolling the concerns of veteran educators, etc.)
>
> This messiah complex compels top-down reforms and resists partnerships with parents and listening to communities because these reformers truly believe they know best. Education reform fueled by martyrdom . . . is missing the mark. One of my mentors, Dr. Gloria Ladson-Billings, said recently, "Catching up is made nearly impossible by our structural inequalities." In agreement with her and with . . . Dr. Ravitch, I believe that until education reform corrects structural inequalities teeming in under-resourced, historically marginalized communities, education reform will continue to fall short of its goal. (Royal, 2012)

Royal's concern about top-down reforms and steamrolling and resisting partnerships with parents and local communities hearkens back to the very dawn of punitive test-based accountability.

Sandy Kress, the father of the movement, was a passionate Democratic businessman in Dallas, Texas. At the request of Yvonne Ewell, one of three African Americans on the Dallas ISD school board, Kress chaired a commission—the Commission on Educational Excellence—that prepared a report calling for improvements to educational quality in the district. Kress's report laid out a simple but novel strategy for obtaining those improvements: rewards and punishments for schools and educators based on student standardized test scores, broken out by subgroups.

"It had never been done before," said one ally of Kress (Donald, 2000).

It started, for Kress, as a "holy crusade to help minority children" (Donald, 2000). It ended, nationally, in a powerful alliance of compassionate liberals, testing corporation lobbyists, and free-market conservatives wringing every last drop of efficiency (and, some would say, hope) out of an entire nation of public school teachers and students.

Kress made his way from the excellence committee and onto the Dallas ISD school board, and he eventually became its president. His stay would end in a mess of raging racial strife. Modern school reform was a steamroller from the beginning. His approach was "heavy-handed" and "aggressive," relying on hardball politics and backroom deals to advance his agenda (Donald, 2000).

"Sandy created a perception that he wasn't interested in what the black community wanted," said one former trustee (Donald, 2000). Blacks viewed him with suspicion, and his term is remembered as "one of the most racially divisive periods in the history of DISD" (Donald, 2000). Ultimately, Kress resigned from the board and moved to Austin, but his commitment to the outcomes-steamroller he had invented never wavered, nor did his belief that the ends justified the means.

Referring to the opposition in the Black community to his messianic ways, Kress once remarked, "I was foggy about it then, and I am foggy about it now" (Donald, 2000).

The Achievement Trap

The great thing about a test-score achievement gap—if you can get past the intrinsic suggestion that White kids' scores are normal and other races' scores are either deficient or exceptional—is that it is easily measured. Its narrowing is a substitute goal for the far more daunting aim of reducing America's hard-baked societal inequalities. Test scores are a facsimile of reality, and narrowing gaps between them is a facsimile of equality.

It is as if Teddy Roosevelt had said, "Digging the Panama Canal is a great idea, but it's really hard to gauge progress because ships aren't sailing through it yet. Let's come up with a substitute for the original goal of getting ships from the West Coast to the East Coast more quickly and safely and measure that. Let's measure how many people are working on the docks in San Francisco and work toward increasing that number."

Never mind the fact that, like test scores, this statistic could be easily influenced by factors other than the completion of the real, original goal of completing the canal. Trade with China could increase, for example.

And never mind that the statistic could be easily inflated through dishonest means by the subjects of rewards and punishments. Dock managers, understanding that the government wanted to see gains, could simply hire new secretaries and call them dock workers on the paperwork.

Roosevelt wasn't opposed to measurement or accountability. To the contrary, the progress of the Panama Canal's construction was routinely publicized both among the workers in Panama and among the readers of American newspapers. Friendly competition among different departments was encouraged to spur progress. But Roosevelt's administrators relied on measurements of progress toward the actual goal—building a canal—and not metrics reflecting alternative, easy-to-fake signals of progress.

The core of the disagreement over school reform is whether racial test score misalignment is a sign of educational failure or a sign of social failure. This disagreement about the root cause seems to be intractable.

The fact that we talk almost exclusively about test score gaps and graduation rates and never talk about all the other gaps that prevail in our society—Black Americans wind up in jail more often, have lower-paying jobs, are more likely to be unemployed, live in more dangerous neighborhoods, have less access to investment capital, and on and on and on—says something really nasty about us. But it also says that as a society, we aren't comfortable attributing the conditions of poor Americans to our social policies and historical choices.

It's easier on us all if we blame bad teachers for poverty instead of race-clumsy lawmakers. After all, we didn't elect the teachers.

While the truth about the cause of our nation's achievement gaps probably lives in the gray area between the two warring education camps—low test scores can and do indicate both bad teaching and an inequitable society—the fact that educational and not social failure today commands the attention of philanthropists and the media hints at a profound moral laziness at the heart of reform. There is a paucity of courage on display when billionaires beat the daylights out of teachers yet treat entrenched inequity with kid gloves.

Standardized tests, as I said once in a speech, are a poor substitute for justice.

The Opportunity Gap

The Opportunity to Learn Campaign[1] in Washington, DC, prefers the term "opportunity gap" to "achievement gap." The achievement gap is merely a symptom of the opportunity gap, a piece of a larger problem that transcends education. The achievement gap is one soft vein in a bigger rock wall that we as a nation need to cut through, and a tiny vein at that, a mere part of the whole, not the whole itself. It draws our attention (and a flurry of hectic reformers with their glinting, high-promise tools) because it's easier to carve at than the rest of the wall. Some of us have convinced ourselves that the rest of the wall isn't there.

Pretending that the hard stuff isn't there doesn't help accomplish the actual, urgent, and nobly daunting goal of getting our nation's beautiful, potential-rich poor children standing on an equal plain of possibility with their privileged neighbors across town. It doesn't do a thing to get East Coast ships into the Pacific waters of the West, to appropriate Roosevelt's bold challenge.

Being self-satisfied with the high-minded firing of city teachers and the experimental provision of private school vouchers or under-regulated charter schools to select city children—the "civil rights issues of our time," as they say—while we ignore all the other civil wrongs plainly in front of our faces, won't get us through this looming wall where we Americans pile up and crush one another. Past American political choices—whether we have the courage to acknowledge it or not—have concentrated character-hollowing conditions in communities where people need the most help and the most, gulp, investment. The inequitable conditions are not only *not* alleviated by modern education reform as it has been popularized, but they are accommodated and excused by it.

Substituting achievement gaps for gaping social wounds as the target of our frantic labors only lets us pretend we are making great progress as we stir up a cloud of dust and make a sound and fury doing it. But the hard things remain—we don't fix them—because progress on test scores is not the same thing as progress.

EIGHT

Compounding Poverty with Inequity

W HEN THE AUTHORS OF *A Nation at Risk* convinced a mass of media and political figures to grab their pitchforks and torches and go single-mindedly after bad teachers, the real monsters—disinvestment and inequity—were left to ravage the town. Business lobbyists were surely thrilled as they watched the angry mob surround the teachers' lounge and chant "No excuses!" The excuses they were shushed from mentioning happened to be quite profitable. Inequity in school funding, for example, is the only mechanism by which our nation's oracles of profit can realistically get away with the tax-reducing gambit of underfunding a historically popular public service like universal schooling.

GOODBYE TO FOOTBALL

E RNEST SINGLETON CAME TO Premont Independent School District as superintendent of schools in June 2012, and a month later received a letter from the Texas Education Agency informing him that the school would be closed. Premont had struggled for years with poor finances and poor student achievement. Singleton begged for a reprieve and was granted a 1-year delay. The delay came with a list of daunting to-dos, including paying down district debts, remodeling insufficient science labs, and improving student attendance.

Money was an issue. It had been for ages in Premont. But Singleton was single-minded and maybe just a little desperate. Facing the abyss, he did what few if any superintendents in Texas have had the temerity (or lunacy) to attempt: He canceled football. Singleton figured the money he saved by cutting out all school athletic and cheerleading programs might be just enough to help him save the school (Smith, 2012a).

Scott Hochberg was a state representative from Houston, widely considered the House's whiz when it came to matters related to school funding. A curious type with a mop of gray hair, Hochberg noticed something about Premont that everyone else had overlooked. As the state's academic accountability system condemned the school for its underperforming students and the state's financial accountability system condemned the school for its fiscal condition, everyone but Hochberg was content to obsess about the district's unacceptable outputs. But Hochberg stole a glance at the inputs and realized something pretty relevant. He noticed that in Texas's inequitable school funding system, Premont was one of the lowest-funded schools in the state, and had been for years. Hochberg presented a graph to the House Education Committee showing them how Texas's Academically Unacceptable school districts had, on average, $1,000 less funding per pupil than the state's Exemplary school districts. In light of Premont's dire straits— and the high-profile cancellation of sports there—Hochberg told a reporter that "the districts that we choose to fund poorly are the districts that we then come down and whip" (Smith, 2012a).

The accountability systems in place in Texas blindly suggested that something was wrong with Premont—with the kids or the teachers or the parents there. And as school rating systems came out year after year, local papers never questioned the conclusions that the Texas Education Agency proclaimed via its powerful school rating regimes. Scott Hochberg teased out the truth, though. Inputs matter. Something was wrong, all right. Something was very wrong with the way Texas chose to finance education in places like Premont and hundreds of other Texas towns and cities.

Hochberg was probably speaking of school districts when he referred to "winners and losers" under the state's accountability system, but he could have said the same thing about the children within those schools. The young men and women of the Premont class of 2012 will never get back their senior year, after all. They'll never be Cowboys and Cowgirls again. While they watched television on Friday nights or drove up the road to watch some other team play, their peers across Texas bathed in the glow of community adulation as they cheered and played their hearts out for themselves, their parents, and their teammates. Football died that year in Premont, but it wasn't the kids or teachers who killed it. It was killed by legislators who saw fit to bless suburban schools with one level of school funding and schools in poor places with millions less.

The Best and Wisest Parents

Politically powerful parents in America's suburbs won't accept inadequate public schooling for their children—they have minimum expectations that just happen to align nicely with Bloom's taxonomy and John Dewey's quote about what the best and wisest parents want for their children; and they have the voices and the votes to realize at least an approximation of those expectations. Suburban public school parents want for their children precisely what author Jonathan Kozol has vividly described as the components of the wonderful education poor children deserve (and *need*, if they are to enter into the full promise of this nation). These parents want their children's schools to have well-appointed libraries, reasonable class sizes, ample time for exploration and play, comfortable climate-controlled buildings, safe surroundings, and green grass.

The only difference is that poor people have little more to cling to than Jonathan Kozol's eloquence; suburbanites have political heft and can actually make sure their children get something approaching their loving standard of educational quality.

The politically powerless can apparently do little to stop the growth of their children's classes, the crumbling of their facilities, the closing of their schools, and the replacing of their certified teachers with temporary interns. Inequity is the mechanism that allows tax resisters to selectively shortchange education and avoid picking a fight with suburban parents who won't hesitate to call elected officials out if they don't take good care of their children, and whose voices are sure to be attended to. Inequity is enabled by results-oriented school reform, as politicians and foundations insist on averting our view from the inputs.

Absent inequity, inadequacy is impossible. And prior to the bleak dawn of punitive reform, inequity was recognized by many as the first enemy of good schooling and a healthy democracy.

Today, you won't hear the most prominent education reformers advocating for equitable school funding. Equality is simply too expensive for the funders backing reform; firing teachers and opening charter schools is their preference. They are all for saving poor Black children, as long as it can be done on the cheap.

The Civil Rights Issue of Our Timid

At the core[1] of this debate is a fight about causation. Academic failure is disproportionately found among poor and minority children.

In Texas, the highest-funded schools get millions of dollars more per year than the lowest-funded schools. The state has very aggressively published the academic results of students in these schools, but it is silent when it comes to reporting the school funding inputs. The "Money doesn't matter" faction of the school reform alliance is also suspiciously quiet when it comes to whether school districts should be asked to get the same results as schools with millions more in funding to play with. Whether they should be asked to do this or not, they *are* asked to do it. This is reality.

Plateau Villa and Workman are two Texas communities of about the same population. Their names have been changed so as not to cause consternation among the inhabitants. The data shared in this section are accurate, however, taken from the U.S. Census and Texas's Academic Excellence Information System (AEIS) reports.[2] Plateau Villa had an average household income of $176,375 between 2005 and 2009. During the same period, Workman's average household income was $39,508. Median home values in the two communities were $982,600 and $80,700, respectively.

The point isn't that there are rich communities and poor communities in America. The point is that one of these two communities (Plateau Villa) gets significantly more per pupil school funding than the other, and it's the one whose students have educational needs that are exponentially less critical and less expensive to remediate.

The rich get a richer education. This might demonstrate the easy path that our politics invariably take, but it doesn't remotely identify what would be pragmatically best for the future well-being of our nation.

The Equity Center[3] in Texas reports that Workman's per pupil target revenue in 2012 was $4,973. Plateau Villa's was $6,013. Both schools had just over 6,000 students.

Texas allots Workman $29,838,000 with which to educate their 6,000 high-poverty students. Meanwhile, the Lone Star State awards Plateau Villa $36,078,000 with which to educate their higher-income pupils, who by all accounts arrived at school having enjoyed "50,000 hours between conception and the first day of kindergarten" that were marked by a great deal of preparation for learning (Bligh, 2013). That's a difference in funding of almost $7 million for those 6,000 pupils.

The outcomes are stark. Plateau Villa is able to pay its teachers, on average, 10% more. Staff turnover at Plateau Villa—where not only is the pay higher, but also the job of inculcating knowledge is most assuredly easier—is half as high.

The student benefits that flow from the higher funding are various. Fifteen percent fewer of Workman's students graduate in 4 years. An astounding 98% of Plateau Villa's students annually pass all of their state tests, compared with 67% of Workman's students. College-ready numbers bear out the same pattern.

Damningly, the school with the smallest challenges is blessed with the most generous resourcing under the Texas funding system, and yet the hyperintense focus of Texas lawmakers for 3 decades has been on holding teachers accountable for good teaching.

Are relentless poverty and indefensible inequality really just "excuses" for teachers? Surely they really do exert a powerful incapacitating influence on the inculcation of knowledge and skills. Couldn't it be for that (unselfish) reason that poverty and inequity provoke an outcry from teachers? Or must education reformers stick to the tired rhetoric that teachers who bring up poverty as a piece of the puzzle are merely looking for an "out" for their own poor performance?

Whether or not the reduction of poverty is a tactic education thinkers should consider as a means of improving outcomes is a key disagreement between nouveau reformers and staid old teachers, and while the reformers are quick to note that teachers have a self-interested motive in blaming poor educational outcomes on poverty (as opposed to their own incompetence), supporters of public education would do well to highlight the fact that education reformers—especially the hedge-funders and billionaires who enjoy the downward pressure inequity applies to their property tax rates—themselves have an embarrassment of self-interest in circling their wagons around poverty, lest it become unpopular enough that costly social reforms dawn as America's way forward.

The modern accountability movement got its start in Dallas ISD in the early 1980s, when Sandy Kress invented the now-ubiquitous system of tests and punishments and disaggregation of data (Donald, 2000). Though he designed the system to improve academic opportunities for poor and minority students in Dallas, his brainchild was immediately embraced by the business community. Meanwhile, Kress and his system eventually earned the scorn of the community he was purporting to serve, resulting in "one of the most tumultuous periods in DISD history" (Pauken, 2013).

Three decades after Kress's magic fix, Texas's school funding system is remarkably inequitable, to the detriment of innumerable children. Disproportionate poverty is considered an unwelcome topic of educational conversation by school reformers. It appears that the unhappy citizens in Dallas were wise to oppose Kress's reforms, as accountability was ultimately marshaled in defense of inequity. We would have done well to listen back then.

"Historically with segregation," noted one retired Dallas ISD board member, reflecting on the first iteration of punitive test-based educational reforms, "when the business community advocates something, it has not been good for blacks" (Donald, 2000).

What We Need Is
More Accountability

If accountability is good for our schools, shouldn't it follow that it is also good for our society? Why are corporate-sponsored foundations and their mouthpieces, incredibly invested as they are in the "civil rights issue of our time," not extending their battle—not employing their finely honed weapons of measurement and consequence—against the equally data-rich fields of social inequity? The punitive school reformers' model of collecting data and deploying punishments based on the improvement in said data, with a particular focus on closing gaps, isn't strictly an educational model. There are racial gaps in the numbers of children who go to bed hungry, not just in the number of children who fail standardized math tests. There are income gaps in the rates of Americans going to prison. What we need are a few punitive *social* reformers crisscrossing the nation and shaking up the unjust status quo.

We don't have failing schools in isolation. Those who bang that drum are confusing cause and effect, whether out of ignorance or duplicity.

Schools fail because society is failing, not vice versa.

We have badly failing equality in our nation today. The data proves it as our income disparities yawn like the Grand Canyon, and yet we allow ourselves to be fooled by those who are extremely selective about which data they agonize over.

Is our nation at risk? Absolutely.

It is at risk of a rising tide of inequality.

We have allowed dishonest arbiters to frighten us with a specter of academic failure, when a real monster called injustice lurks at the foot of our bed—emboldened to the point where it feels no compulsion to hide in the closet.

Fear is the misdirection that has emboldened the eager disequalizers in our society, those who benefit from inequality.

Strangely, none of the liberal advocates for school reform—today's self-declared civil rights leaders—are pushing for no-excuses equality.

Teachers uniquely merit the modern justice-fighter's ire. In fact, so-called no-excuses reform is in practice all excuses when one leaves school property. Racism, poverty, income inequality—it's all just hunky-dory. Too many intrepid reformers call these tragic facts of American life "excuses" and lack the willpower to accept them as challenges for us as a people to confront directly.

Are we to believe that our educational system is guilty and our finance and political and criminal justice and economic systems are innocent?

The truth is, a durable American injustice that we can't bring ourselves to confess incapacitates both teacher and learner. Our public policy—not merely our educational policy—needs a close look. Policymakers need to be held to account for the effectiveness of their decisions in assuring children—all children—an equal opportunity to learn.

The simple erection of high hurdles in front of our teachers and kids will not help them fly if they are chained to the ground by unequal treatment. There is a diabolical lie at the heart of school reform that must be refuted.

Poverty *does* matter.

Inequality is *not* inevitable. Horrendous life conditions matter. Desperation in the home that precludes careful parenting defers dreams and stunts educational attainment. Under the shock therapy of reform, terrified teachers may try desperately to push the accelerator through the floorboard, but the engine still won't burn the water our society allows to seep into the gas tank of education.

But it is easier to blame the driver than it is to fix the car. It is hard—but it is ultimately patriotic—to repair our vehicle. Teachers aren't mules to carry children; our democracy was supposed to be the vehicle to propel us all toward a better future. The rhetoricians love to claim that teachers are saying, "Fix poverty before you hold me accountable." That's a lie. Teachers are simply saying, "Don't let poverty run free."

That's it. Do it. The world is watching, and it won't be long before the world realizes it isn't the teachers who are making excuses.

The Best American Day

The roots of our injustice will at length find themselves in the cross-hairs of the unrestricted, undiffused ire of the American people. Each new generation is more accepting than the last of neighbors of different colors and diverse backgrounds. And the demographics of the nation are shifting as quickly as its attitudes. Radio blather will ultimately fall on ears that can't hear it over the din of poor children's clamoring for more decent American lives. Squalor will not forever be held back by the gates of our gated communities.

The attention of conservatives and liberals alike, of Southerners and Northerners, of rural Americans and urban Americans and Americans in between will on that best American day align and be fixed squarely in the direction of the most basic causal agent of every last one of our greatest national challenges: persistent inequality that benefits a select (and vociferous) few.

We will on that day be possessed of an uncommon unity not unlike that previously inspired by grave and sudden national crises; and this one is certainly grave if not sudden. We will finally see injustice clearly for what it is, the amalgamation of more violence and pain and loss and unfairness than all of our abrupt historical cataclysms combined, spread out over generations and miles and many millions of victims, a slow drip of concentrated social toxins that poison an entire nation's freedom and prosperity by withering its most defenseless children's opportunities. It is our cultural pollution.

But on that day our national pride will demand that our spines stiffen and our efforts coalesce. That will be the day when we will all finally be judged by the content of our character and not prejudged by the economic circumstances of our birth.

The Fundamental Enemy of Academic Achievement

The enemy, then, of academic achievement in poor America is not the failing teacher. It is the failing citizen. Every actor whose fingerprints are on these children is at fault. The teacher takes the blame because the rest of us too often go easy on ourselves, even as we pull the lever in the voting booth that condemns our poorest children into the hands of men and women more interested in the good of cronies than the well-being of needy children. Lawmakers in many states casually invest millions more educating kids in rich neighborhoods than they spend educating kids in poor neighborhoods. Somehow they sleep at night, knowing that the teeth of the machine they've built chew up poor children who will inevitably become brittle adults.

Our votes create these circumstances that we have blessed with our silence.

The correlation between poverty and academic failure is direct. "Money doesn't matter" is merely a talking point clung to by those unwilling to consider the price of needed repairs in light of our nation's historical social vandalisms.

Wraparound services that work to reduce the acuteness of societal impairments are the Nikes in this track race. Poor children can indeed run like the wind, but we ask them to run barefoot. When parents fail at basic parenting and government fails at basic governing, it necessarily falls to the voters, in their own best interest, to give to all children what the wisest and best parents give to theirs: proper health care, early exposure to language and numeracy, experiences that promote productive enterprise, minimum expectations for self-uplifting behaviors, and so many other things. If we as a people are unwilling to step in and save floundering children, then we will get what we deserve. We must be willing to pay the price of maintaining the children we choose to neglect when they become flawed adults.

We don't fix things because it costs more than we are willing to spend.

A truly strong country is made of people who exhibit the courage of caring for other people's children, including and especially those who are different than them, even if the cost is dear.

✪ NINE ✪

The Prescription Has Failed

We stand at a daunting threshold and on the other side see a world of free market, unregulated schools. The richest people in America are enamored at the possibilities that this future holds for them. The dangers it poses to our cultural and religious minorities and to our students with special needs—dangers of exclusion, mistreatment, and unaccountability—are legion. A gaping maw awaits them in the de-democratized future of American education.

This leering threat calls for a new report, an *A Nation at Risk 2* that outlines the potential devastation we are preparing to inflict on our republic. The death of public education—eagerly pined for by a powerful few—is nothing nobler than the slamming shut of our widest door in the faces of those who need it opened. It is the opposite of the inspirational verses inscribed on our Statue of Liberty, saying essentially, "Send elsewhere your poor and hurting."

I will end, though, not with a jeremiad about the fearful things that may lie ahead, but with a hopeful rebuke to the lies that got us here. Our nation isn't at risk; it is pregnant with blessed promise. What the authors of that infamous 1983 report should have done in the first place was to survey all that is right and hopeful in our education system and to offer prescriptions for making what is working for so many, work for all. But ideology trumped our national good, and the opportunity to sow fear and reap hysterics was too tempting. We have, in American education, run off into a bog.

A Nation of Promise

I offer, then, the following six solutions.

1. Implement Universal Pre-K for Poor Children. A recent spate of studies cited by Eduardo Porter in the *New York Times* showed that cognitive gaps observed in small children change very little as they age (2013). The same article shows that, compared with countries like Australia, Sweden, and Germany, the United States spends a paltry amount of its GDP on early childhood education. In fact, we spend over 60% of our education dollars on later years of secondary education, when disadvantages have calcified, and less than 10% on infants and toddlers. Meanwhile, research cited by Porter "confirms that investment in the early education of disadvantaged children pays extremely high returns down the road. It improves not only their cognitive abilities but also crucial behavioral traits like sociability, motivation and self-esteem" (2013).

Fortunately, President Obama seemed to embrace the importance of early childhood education when he used his 2013 State of the Union Address to call for providing universal pre-K for every 4-year-old from lower-income homes. "Let's make sure none of our kids start out the race of life a step behind," he said later, while explaining his initiative to a group of teachers in Georgia (Sink, 2013).

It might even be worth considering, as some (including one-time Dallas ISD superintendent Linus Wright[1]) have suggested, getting rid of the 12th grade altogether and instead making pre-K mandatory for all students.

2. Remove Property Worth as a Factor in School Funding. In many states, students in America's poorest neighborhoods have been condemned to a second-rate public education—despite the facile assurances of school reformers—not simply because of instructional failures of their teachers, but because of structural failures of the school funding system. These students often receive lower levels of funding for their learning, which translates directly into lower-paid teachers, fewer instructional materials, older and sparser technological supports, older and less-comfortable buildings, larger class sizes, and fewer and more poorly equipped extracurricular and remedial programs. These things matter.

Yet, as long as property-value-driven funding mechanisms ensure that a large number of upper-middle-class parents see high-quality public schools in their neighborhoods, there will be insufficient pressure on legislators to provide more funding in low-property-value areas where it is most needed.

The funding of schools in America's poorest neighborhoods must be tied to formulas driven by the actual cost of educating enrolled students rather than property values, or else we are ourselves putting the "generational" in generational poverty.

3. Enlist Better Gatekeepers in Educator Preparation Programs. Entry requirements such as SAT scores for teacher preparation programs should be raised so that teaching as a field evolves into a more exclusive career path. This simple squeeze in the pipeline would drive up the quality of teaching candidates and would reduce teacher supply, and as a result, drive up compensation. Alternative certification programs must also be monitored to ensure quality. These changes would do more to improve the quality of the American teaching corps than all the mean-spirited, scientifically questionable, autonomy-crushing tactics reformers have put forth, and would do so without further demoralizing the great teachers we have bleeding in the trenches today.

Education expert Pasi Sahlberg has noted that carefully guarding teacher quality was one of the crucial factors that led to the exemplary performance of Finland's education system (Hattie, n.d.). The United States would do well to follow suit. It isn't necessary to tie teachers' evaluations to student test scores using experimental value-added formulas of dubious scientific validity because, like Finland, we can nudge our best and brightest into teaching, and then we can return to an era in which educators were trusted with education.

4. Use Testing for Diagnostic, Not Punitive Purposes. Data-informed school leadership is a boon for children, but excessively punitive and coercive systems built atop testing data are a perverting force that contorts the wholesome enterprise of teaching children into a bloodthirsty race. This is the great horror of what we have done, scarier in reality than the most over-the-top proclamations in *A Nation at Risk*. This damaging educational approach must be shunned by history.

5. Reject Any Accountability Formula That Doesn't Mathematically Factor Context. If schools are to be given targets—whether they be graduation rates, test scores, college-going percentages, or what have you—those schools' progress toward said targets should be weighed squarely in the context of the manifold factors surrounding the school. There should never again be a school accountability system that expects a school funded at half the per-pupil allotment of neighboring districts to achieve identical performance-based results. That the plain injustice of this goes unchallenged boggles the fair mind. If there is to be inequity in circumstance at the start of the race—not that there should be a race at all—then we must accept inequity in the expected outcomes.

By leaving poverty out of accountability, and by leaving inequity out of accountability, we have deliberately shut off spotlights that might otherwise spur us to restorative action. We have satisfied ourselves to shout "Bad schools," and there are no words left to condemn injustice.

6. Amplify Teachers' and Students' Voices in Policy. Teachers should be professionalized and trusted to design the evaluation systems and the accountability systems put in place to judge their profession. Students' voices should likewise not be shut out. It's time for student councils to do more than sell T-shirts, and it's time for teachers to do more than help design test questions for Pearson, PLC. The policies must be driven by practitioners and real—not pretend—stakeholders.

Governmental committees established to make decisions about accountability are often comprised of business elites and—at least in Texas—Pearson's lobbyists, with perhaps some token teachers on board, but with no real voice. Recently in Texas, the state's education commissioner told the Senate Education Committee that he was implementing an A–F grading system for schools because it was recommended to him. Strangely, an advisory committee comprised of educators recommended *against* that very system, and the question arose: Who recommended it? The commissioner hasn't answered that question as of this writing, but it's been reported that one member of the committee did speak up in favor of the idea—the head of the Texas Association of Business (Stanford, 2013). It appears that a lone business voice held veto power over an entire committee of daily-involved educational stakeholders.

In New York, as tests tied to the new Common Core State Standards hit student desks for the first time, a professor at Teachers College at Columbia University named Lucy Calkins set up a website eliciting feedback from teachers as well as parents regarding the tests. The responses were both legion and "overwhelmingly negative" (Layton, 2013). Calkins, an author who had written in support of the Common Core Standards, was taken aback. "I'm a big supporter of the Common Core," she said. "But this makes even me question it" (Layton, 2013).

Teachers' voices are important in the design of education policy, but because the conclusions of teachers—who see reforms play out in their classrooms—often do not align with the goals of reformers, they are often ignored or, in some cases, completely avoided. In December 2012, a secret group calling itself the "skunk works" began meeting in Michigan. It included aides to Governor Rick Snyder and had the goal of creating "value schools," which could be run at a reduced cost compared to traditional schools. The team included at least one well-known proponent of school vouchers and precisely one teacher, the 2011 Michigan Educator of the Year. The teacher left the group, however, when he realized its discussions centered on "a special kind of school being created outside of the Michigan public school system" (Livengood, 2013). Presumably, the group absent its lone educator continued to generate plans for the future of education in the state of Michigan, and to do so with absolutely no input from the people most knowledgeable about the field this group was fiddling with.

As long as teachers and students are left out of the policy decisions that affect them more than anyone, they will continue to seek and find alternative means of letting their voices be heard. Save Our Schools rallies, teacher strikes, opt-out movements, and student walk-outs will be a growing reality as long as genuine influence in policy development is denied to those most impacted. The new cry of teachers and students might be "No reform without representation" as they struggle for input into the nation-building task in which they invest their lives.

Removing the voices of teachers and students from conversations about how to hold schools accountable has resulted in a national epidemic of clumsy, ill-fitting, ineffective practices being shoehorned into place by bureaucrats and businesspeople who either meant well or, in some cases, meant to just blow things up. It never had to be this way: Mistrusting educators and those educated by them was a conscious choice; restricting their input into educational decisions was a calculated decision, and a very bad one.

As school accountability led by a coalition of overconfident business lobbyists and politicians went haywire in Texas, a group of concerned superintendents began meeting and planning for the future. The result was first a statement of principles and then a piece of legislation that established the Texas High Performance Schools Consortium. This coalition of school people was tasked with designing a new method of holding schools accountable; it was, as one member of the consortium put it, "the research and development process for the future" (Gilbert, 2013). Several "outside entities" had been entrusted for years with the development of accountability and assessment practices in Texas public schools, and "the reality of letting non-Texas education professionals take the lead in assessment and accountability" led to a progressively unwieldy and unpopular system that became almost universally despised by teachers and parents (Gilbert, 2013). (The same system, of course, went national and became No Child Left Behind, and then was despised from coast to coast.)

Many public education activists have noted that doctors and lawyers determine accountability standards for their own professions and have recommended that the same be true in education.

The Texas High Performance Schools Consortium is, as of this writing, developing a system with features like multiple meaningful measures of student learning, an electronic portfolio of work samples used as evidence of mastery (as opposed to a single bubble test score), local accountability for results, and the creation of a "21st century learning environment for every student" (Gilbert, 2013).

Educators bring a perspective to reform that is sorely lacking nationwide. Reform should be done by educators, not to them.

"Fear and learning" has been America's ascetic education religion for 3 decades. Churn and change have been relentless, and fearful recriminations for educators and students have been the order of the day—ever-increasing in volume and ferocity. Nevertheless, despite many miracle prescriptions and all sorts of efforts by some of America's richest people in the face of the misleading diagnosis, the people who were saying our schools were terrible in 1983 are still saying the same thing today. American public schools, it can be argued, will be deemed failing in certain quarters no matter what.

Scary stories, however, lose their frightfulness with time and repetition. The menacing doom predicted in 1983 never came to fruition—kids who were in high school then are in their late 40s or early 50s today, and America's "once unchallenged preeminence in commerce, industry, science, and technological innovation" still hasn't been "overtaken by competitors throughout the world" (National Commission on Excellence in Education, 1983).

The wolf, it turns out, isn't really killing the sheep.

It never was.

✪ APPENDIX ✪

A Layperson's Guide for Involved Teachers, Students, and Parents

The corporate education reform movement is not only well-financed but also well-organized and well-connected. To paraphrase Diane Ravitch, they have the money, but those who support public education have overwhelming numbers on their side. Those numbers equal votes, and votes speak loudly to elected officials, perhaps even more loudly than the campaign contributions of billionaires who want to remake America's schools in Wall Street's increasingly grotesque image.

Those who would resist the most abusive of the privatizers' aims in education would do well to unite and agitate en masse. This approach worked well in Texas in 2013 when—with a number of aggressive pro-schools grassroots organizations pressing hard on legislators and actively informing the public of reform's failings via rallies, town halls, and letters to the editor—standardized testing was reduced significantly in scope and stakes for the first time ever, after the unanimous passage of House Bill 5.

In the beginning of this book, I referred to the dangers associated with advocacy for teachers, and in this Appendix I want to share resources that will allow teachers to advocate for and stay informed about the fight over public education, often with the anonymity that the web can provide. These resources are not only for teachers but also for politically active parents and students who, because of the vulnerability of teachers, are invaluable to the effort to preserve public education because they can often speak plainly and can't be dismissed by corporate reformers as people merely feathering their own nests.

The resources referenced here are presented in sections:

- national public education advocacy organizations
- state-based public education advocacy organizations
- journalists and journals
- blogs and other online sources of information
- fair-minded films about public education

Some advocacy organizations below are involved in other areas in addition to education, but I listed them if I felt their education focus was a significant part of what they do. It is important to note, too, that not all of the organizations listed agree on every single educational policy, and not all public education supporters will align with every organization on every point. It is important for teachers, parents, and students who want to get involved to find the organizations that fit their personalities and political leanings. The defense of public education is neither a Democratic nor a Republican imperative; there is room on the front lines for everyone who cares about public education and wants to see it survive in America. There is room in the movement for suburban moms who see the damage test-centered educational approaches and underfunding are having on their children's education. There is room for urban dads who worry about school closures and charter co-locations. Some groups listed primarily oppose the misuse of testing. Others are most concerned about inequity in funding. Still others focus on opposing private school vouchers.

Many disparate (but equally misguided) policy priorities have coalesced to form the presently dominant corporate education agenda, and the best approach for those who wish to effect positive change in the face of the onslaught is an inclusive one. These resources, then, are intended as a menu for a budding public schools activist—I hope invigorated and poised to get involved—to carefully choose from.

My advice to those concerned about the future of public education is to get involved in some way and be part of the struggle to save our public schools. Learn about the issues and use your teacher voice, parent voice, or student voice. Write letters to the editor in your local paper if you are so inclined. Post commentaries and links to relevant journalism on Twitter or Facebook. Tell your friends. Fight the reform wars in the comments sections of reform-friendly blogs. Challenge misconceptions and deliberate mendacity when you have the chance. Spread the news each time public schools do something well, and spread the news each time yet another reform initiative is proven fraudulent.

The fight for public education is nothing more, ultimately, than a tug-of-war with public opinion. The American public will either believe in their schools, or they will lose faith.

So speak up. Even if you must use a pseudonym to do it.

Selected National Public Education Advocacy Organizations

Advancement Project—safequalityschools.org
Broader, Bolder Campaign—boldapproach.org
Change the Stakes—changethestakes.wordpress.com
Class Size Matters—classsizematters.org
Education Opportunity Network—educationopportunitynetwork.org
Equal Schools Educational Non-Profit—equalschools.com
FairTest—fairtest.org
First Focus—firstfocus.net
Great Schools for America—greatschoolsforamerica.org
K12 News Network—K12NewsNetwork.com
Learning First Alliance—learningfirst.org
National Opportunity to Learn Campaign (OTL)—otlcampaign.org
Network for Public Education (NPE)—networkforpubliceducation.org
Parents Across America (PAA)—parentsacrossamerica.org
Parents United for Responsible Education (PURE)—pureparents.org
Save Our Schools (SOS)—saveourschoolsmarch.org
Students United for Public Education—studentsunitedforpubliced.org
United Opt Out National—unitedoptout.com
Voices for Education—voicesforeducation.org

Selected State-Based Advocacy Organizations

CALIFORNIA

The Sacramento Coalition to Save Public Education—
   savesacramentopublicschools.org

COLORADO

Coalition for Better Education—thecbe.org
DeFENSE—defensedenver.com
Taxpayers for Public Education—taxpayersforpubliceducation.org

FLORIDA

Chris Guerrieri's Education Matters—jaxkidsmatter.blogspot.com
Testing Is Not Teaching—facebook.com/testingisnotteaching

ILLINOIS

More Than a Score—morethanascorechicago.org
Raise Your Hand—ilraiseyourhand.org

INDIANA

Indiana Coalition for Public Education—icpe2011.com
Northeast Indiana Friends of Public Education—neifpe.blogspot.com

Michigan

Michigan Parents for Schools—mipfs.org
Protecting Public Education in Michigan—ppemichigan.wordpress.com

Minnesota

Public Education Justice Alliance of Minnesota—pejamn.blogspot.com

Missouri

Missouri Education Watchdog—missourieducationwatchdog.com

Nevada

Nevada Education Coalition—nved.org

New Hampshire

Advancing New Hampshire Public Education—anhpe.org

New Jersey

Defend New Jersey Public Education—facebook.com/DefendNJEd
Save Our Schools New Jersey—facebook.com/SaveOurSchoolsNJ

New York

The Coalition for Public Education—forpubliced.org
NYC Public School Parents—nycpublicschoolparents.blogspot.com
Parent Voices NY—parentvoicesny.org
Western New Yorkers for Public Education—wnyforpubliced.weebly.com

North Carolina

Public Schools First NC—publicschoolsfirstnc.org

Oregon

Oregon SOS—facebook.com/OregonSaveOurSchools

Pennsylvania

Great Public Schools (GPS) Pittsburgh—facebook.com/
    GreatPublicSchoolsPittsburgh
Keystone State Education Coalition—keystonestateeducationcoalition.
    blogspot.com
Parents United for Public Education—parentsunitedphila.com

Rhode Island

Providence Student Union—providencestudentunion.org

Tennessee

Schooling Memphis—schoolingmemphis.blogspot.com

TEXAS

Equity Center—equitycenter.org
Friends of Texas Public Schools—fotps.org
Make Education a Priority—schoolpriority.com
Raise Your Hand Texas—raiseyourhandtexas.org
Save Texas Schools—savetxschools.org
Speak Up for Texas Public Schools—facebook.com/
 SpeakUpforTexasPublicSchools
Texans Advocating for Meaningful Student Assessment (TAMSA)—tamsatx.org
Texas Kids Can't Wait—texaskidscantwait.org
Texas Parent PAC—txparentpac.com

WASHINGTON

Seattle Schools Community Forum—saveseattleschools.blogspot.com

Selected Journalists and Journals
(may cover more than education)

Lee Fang (@lhfang)
Dana Goldstein (@danagoldstein)
Patti Kilday Hart (@pattihart)
John Merrow (@john_merrow)
Abby Rapoport (@rarapoport)
Joy Resmovits (@joy_resmovits)
Rethinking Schools (rethinkingschools.org)

Motoko Rich (@motokorich)
Stephanie Simon (@stephaniesimon)
David Sirota (@davidsirota)
Morgan Smith (@morgansmith)
Jason Stanford (@jasstanford)
Greg Toppo (@gtoppo)
Michael Winerip (@winerip)

Blogs, Websites, and Online Publications
(Twitter handles in parentheses, when known)

AlfieKohn.org (@alfiekohn)
Atthechalkface.com (various authors)
Bigeducationape.blogspot.com
Blogs.edweek.org/edweek/bridging-
 differences/ (@debmeier)
Blogs.edweek.org/teachers/living-in-
 dialogue (@anthonycody)
Blogs.edweek.org/teachers/teacher-
 in-a-strange-land)
 (@nancyflanagan)
Bloom-at.blogspot.com
Bobsidlethoughtsandmusings.
 wordpress.com

Childrenaremorethantestscores.
 blogspot.com (@readdoctor)
CloakingInequity.com
 (@ProfessorJVH)
Crazycrawfish.wordpress.com
 (@crazycrawfish)
Dailyhowler.blogspot.com
 (@thedailyhowler)
Dangerouslyirrelevant.org (@mcleod)
DeborahMeier.com (@debmeier)
Deutsch29.wordpress.com
Dianeravitch.net (@dianeravitch)
Editbarry.wordpress.com (@editbarry)

Ednotesonline.com (@normscott1)
Educarenow.wordpress.com
    (@billboyle24)
Educatefortexas.com (@drjerryburkett)
Edushyster.com (@edushyster)
Edutalknola.com (@KHRoyal)
Garyrubinstein.teachforus.org
    (@garyrubinstein)
HuffingtonPost.com/news/@
    education123/
Iamaneducator.com (@jessehagopian)
Idea.org
Laststand4children.com
    (@LS4C1.com)
Learning.blogs.nytimes.com
JerseyJazzman.blogspot.com
    (@jerseyjazzman)
Joebower.org (@joe_bower)
JonathanPelto.com (@jonathanpelto)
Kenmlibby.com (@kenmlibby)
Larryferlazzo.edublogs.org
    (@larryferlazzo)
Mothercrusader.blogspot.com
    (@MotherCrusader)
Nepc.colorado.edu (@nepctweet)
NYCdoenuts.blogspot.com
    (@nycdoenuts)
PasiSahlberg.com/category/English
    (@pasi_sahlberg)

PeterMDewitt.com (@PeterMDewitt)
Reclaimreform.com
Roundtheinkwell.com
    (@carolburris)
SabrinaJoyStevens.com
    (@teachersabrina)
SamChaltain.com (@samchaltain)
Schoolfinance101.wordpress.com
    (@schlfinance101)
Sdkrashen.com (@skrashen)
Shankerblog.org (@shankerinst)
Spaceforlearning.wordpress.com
    (@pammoran)
StudentsLast.blogspot.com
    (@studentslast)
Teacherunderconstruction.com
    (@stephrrivera)
Ted.com/talks
Theeducatorsroom.com
    (@educatorsroom)
Thejosevilson.com (@thejlv)
Washingtonpost.com/blogs/
    answersheet (@valeriestrauss)
Withabrooklynaccent.blogspot.com
    (@mcfiredogg)
Yinzercation.wordpress.com
    (@Yinzercation)
Zhaolearning.com
    (@YongZhaoUO)

Public Education Films and Film Projects
(with a Different Perspective than *Waiting for "Superman"*)

180 Days: A Year Inside an American High School (mini-series) (2013)
American Teacher (2011)
August to June: Bringing Life to School (2011)
A Year at Mission Hill (miniseries) (2013)
Go Public: A Documentary Film Project (2012)
The Inconvenient Truth Behind Waiting for "Superman" (2011)
Listen: The Film (in development)
Race to Nowhere (2009)
The Teacher Film (in development)

✪ ✪ ✪

Notes

Chapter 1

1. The target funding number for each district is actually "per WADA" rather than "per pupil." WADA stands for a school's "weighted average daily attendance." To arrive at the WADA for a school district, the state divides the school's number of student days in attendance by the number of school days, and it applies special weights for student groups (special education students and career and technology students, for example, are weighted more than students not involved in those programs). I use "per pupil" for ease of explanation and to prevent the conversation from getting bogged down in the details of the formulas.

Chapter 2

1. All student, educator, and parent names have been changed to protect privacy.

Chapter 3

1. Certain details of Alex's story have been changed to protect his identity.

2. A version of this section originally appeared at theeducatorsroom.com under the title "Contextual Accountability." Reprinted here with permission.

Chapter 4

1. Certain details of Manuel's story have been changed to protect his and his family's identities.

Chapter 7

1. Full disclosure: I serve on the Advisory Board of the Opportunity to Learn Campaign.

Chapter 8

1. A longer treatment of this topic appeared in two parts at Anthony Cody's "Living in Dialogue" blog at *Education Week* in early 2012. The links are blogs. edweek.org/teachers/living-in-dialogue/2012/01/john_kuhn_on_education_ funding.html and blogs.edweek.org/teachers/living-in-dialogue/2012/02/john_ kuhn_america_stop_making.html

2. The AEIS reports for all Texas school districts can be found at ritter.tea.state. tx.us/perfreport/aeis/index.html

3. Infuriatingly, you will not find the list of Target Revenue funding levels anywhere on the Texas Education Agency website. They offer ample data about almost every topic, but the comparative per-student funding levels of each school can only be accessed, as far as I have been able to find, by requesting the information from The Equity Center at equitycenter.org

CHAPTER 9

1. An article about Wright's proposal appeared in the *Dallas Morning News* in 2012. It is found online at dallasnews.com/news/columnists/steve-blow/20120118-former-disd-superintendent-linus-wright-has-bold-plan-for-restructuring-public-education.ece

✪ ✪ ✪

References

Aesop. (n.d.). The Boy Who Cried Wolf. Available at www.eastoftheweb.com/short-stories/UBooks/BoyCri.shtml

Armario, C. (2010, December 7). "Wake-Up Call": U.S. Students Trail Global Leaders. Available at www.nbcnews.com/id/40544897/ns/us_news-life/t/wake-up-call-us-students-trail-global-leaders/

A Timeline of AIDS. (n.d.). Available at aids.gov/hiv-aids-basics/hiv-aids-101/aids-timeline/

Austin, L., & Castro, A. (2006, May 7). Disagreement Over Wealth Sharing Could Derail Special Session. Available at texasedequity.blogspot.com/2006/05/disagreement-over-wealth-sharing-could.html

Bennett, I. (1915). History of the Panama Canal. Available at www.czbrats.com/Builders/Bennett/sanitary.htm

Berliner, D. C., & Biddle, B. J. (1995). *The manufactured crisis: Myths, fraud, and the attack on America's public schools.* New York, NY: Perseus Books.

Bishop, J. (1989). Why the Apathy in American High Schools? Available at www.digitalcommons.ilr.cornell.edu/cgi/viewcontent.cgi?article=1030&context=articles

Bligh, R. (2013, May 9). Poverty and Student Achievement: Are We Comparing the Wrong Groups? Available at www.washingtonpost.com/blogs/answer-sheet/wp/2013/05/09/poverty-and-student-achievement-are-we-comparing-the-wrong-groups/

Bracey, G. (2003, April). April foolishness: The 20th anniversary of *A Nation at Risk. Phi Delta Kappan, 84*(8), 616–621.

Brill, S. (2011, August 13). Super Teachers Alone Can't Save Our Schools. *The Wall Street Journal.* Available at online.wsj.com/article/SB10001424053111903918104576500531066414112.html

Brokaw, T. (1998). *The greatest generation.* New York, NY: Random House.

Calef, R. (n.d.). *More wonders of the invisible world, or the wonders of the invisible world displayed. In five parts.* Charleston, SC: Bibliolife, LLC.

Daley, D. (2012, November 21). Joe Scarborough to Nate Silver: "I'm sorry." Available at www.salon.com/2012/11/21/joe_scarborough_to_nate_silver_im_sorry/

DeYoung, K. (2006, October 1). Falling on His Sword. *Washington Post.* Available at www.washingtonpost.com/wp-dyn/content/article/2006/09/27/AR2006092700106.html

Di Carlo, M. (2012, February 16). If Newspapers Are Going to Publish Teachers' Value-Added Scores, They Need to Publish Error Margins Too. Available at shankerblog.org/?p=5087

Donald, M. (2000, October 19). The Resurrection of Sandy Kress. *Dallas Observer News*. Available at www.dallasobserver.com/2000-10-19/news/the-resurrection -of-sandy-kress/full/

Dwyer, L. (2013, January 9). Data King Nate Silver Isn't Sold on Evaluating Teachers with Test Scores. Available at www.good.is/posts/data-king-nate-silver-isn't -sold-on-evaluating-teachers-with-test-scores

Fisher, M. (2013, April 15). Map: How 35 Countries Compare on Child Poverty (the U.S. Is Ranked 34th). *The Washington Post*. Available at www. washingtonpost.com/blogs/worldviews/wp/2013/04/15/map-how-35-countries-compare-on-child-poverty-the-u-s-is-ranked-34th/

Fletcher, D. (2009, December 11). Standardized Testing. *Time*. Available at www.time. com/time/nation/article/0,8599,1947019,00.html

Friends of Texas Public Schools. (2012). *The blueberry man named 2012 Texas public schools friend of the year*. Available at www.fotps.org/foy2012.php

Gentilviso, R. (2010, August 11). Klein Explains Drop in State Test Scores. *The Queens Gazette*. Available at www.qgazette.com/news/2010-08-11/Features/Klein_ Explains_Drop_In_State_Test_ Scores.html

Gilbert, M. (2013). A Pathway Towards a New System for Accountability. *Longview News-Journal*. Available at www.news-journal.com/opinion/forum/gilbert-a-pathway-towards-a-new-system-for-accountability/article_5a450663-816c-5250-a2ba-6186d7e14194.html

Gioja, Z., & O'Connor, H. (2012, July 4). Texas Scientists Regret Loss of Higgs Boson Quest. Available at www.texastribune.org/2012/07/04/higgs-boson-discovery-may-have-been-possible-texas/

Greatest Historical Ransom. (n.d.). Available at www.guinnessworldrecords.com/ world-records/3000/greatest-historical-ransom.

Grissom, B. (2011a, November 17). Williamson Prosecutor Asserts a Change of Heart. *New York Times*. Available at www.nytimes.com/2011/11/18/us/williamson-prosecutor-john-bradley-has-a-change-of-heart.html?pagewanted=all%22%20 %5Co%20%22Times%20article

Grissom, B. (2011b, December 26). Murder Cases Put "Junk Science" in the Spotlight. Available at www.texastribune.org/texas-dept-criminal-justice/michael-morton/ murder-cases-put-questionable-evidence-trial/

Halperin, A. (2012, December 5). Nate Silver: Still Not Trusted. Available at www.salon. com/2012/12/05/nate_silverstill_not_trusted/

Hatamiya, L. (1999). Institutions and Interest Groups: Understanding the Passage of the Japanese American Redress Bill. In R. Brooks (Ed.), *When sorry isn't enough: The controversy over apologies and reparations for human injustice* (pp. 190–200). New York, NY: New York University Press.

Hattie, J. (n.d.). Interview: Finnish Education Guru Pasi Sahlberg: Treat Primary School Teachers Like Doctors. Available at uncollected-luke.blogspot.com/2012/09/ interview-finnish-education-guru-pasi.html

Haertel, E. H. (2013). Reliability and Validity of Inferences About Teachers Based on Student Test Scores. Available at www.ets.org/s/pdf/23497_Angoff%20Report-web.pdf?utm_content=bufferd18e9&utm_source=buffer&utm_medium= twitter&utm_campaign=Buffer#

Heritage Foundation. (2012, April 11). No They Can't: Why Government Fails—But Individuals Succeed. Available at www.heritage.org/events/2012/04/no-they-cant

Illinois Tool Works, Inc. (2011). History. *Spray Nine*. Available at www.spraynine.com/

content/history

Kamenetz, A. (2013, June 17). News Corp. Introduces a New Kind of Interactivity to the Classroom. *Fast Company.* Available at www.fastcompany.com/3012484/news-corp-amplify

Katyal, N. (2011, May 20). Confession of Error: The Solicitor General's Mistakes During the Japanese-American Internment Cases. Available at blogs.justice.gov/main/archives/1346

Kerchner, C. (2010, September 26). *Waiting for "Superman's"* Half-Truths and Heroes Can Move You to Tears. Available at toped.svefoundation.org/2010/09/26/supermans-half-truths-can-move-you-to-tears/

Kidd, T. (2012, August 9). Lost Confidence. *World Magazine.* Available at www.worldmag.com/2012/08/lost_confidence.

Kirp, D. (2013, April 4). An Urban School District That Works—Without Miracles or Teach for America. Available at www.washingtonpost.com/blogs/answer-sheet/wp/2013/04/04/an-urban-school-district-that-works-without-miracles-or-superman/

Kornblut, E., & Wilson, S. (2011, January 26). State of the Union 2011: "Win the Future," Obama Says. *Washington Post.* Available at www.washingtonpost.com/wp-dyn/content/article/2011/01/25/AR2011012504068.html

Lamare, J. (2012, December 1). Lamare: How Gallup Missed the Mark—Again. *The Detroit News.* Available at www.detroitnews.com/article/20121201/OPINION01/212010312/1008/opinion01/

Layton, L. (2013, April 29). Turmoil Swirling Around Common Core Education Standards. *The Washington Post.* Available at www.washingtonpost.com/local/education/turmoil-swirling-around-common-core-education-standards/2013/04/29/7e2b0ec4-b0fd-11e2-bbf2-a6f9e9d79e19_story.html

Livengood, C. (2013, April 19). Education Reform Group Forges Voucher-Like Plan for Michigan. *The Detroit News.* Available at www.detroitnews.com/article/20130419/SCHOOLS/304190361/Education-reform-group-forges-voucher-like-plan-Michigan?odyssey=tab|topnews|text|FRONTPAGE

Marketing: How to Play the AIDS Scare. (1995, April 2). *Newsweek.* Available at www.thedailybeast.com/newsweek/1995/04/02/marketing-how-to-play-the-aids-scare.html

Mather, C. (1689). Memorable Providences, Relating to Witchcrafts and Possessions. Available at law2.umkc.edu/faculty/projects/ftrials/salem/asa_math.htm

Medina, J. (2010, October 10). On New York School Tests, Warning Signs Ignored. *New York Times.* Available at www.nytimes.com/2010/10/11/education/11scores.html?pagewanted=all

Michelle Rhee Appears on *Meet the Press,* Unveiling StudentsFirst Ad Highlighting Need for Ed Reform. (2012, July 22). Available at www.studentsfirst.org/press/entry/michelle-rhee-appears-on-meet-the-press-unveiling-students-first-ad-highlighting_need_for_ed_reform

Mingle, J. (2012, December 7). Scientists Ask Blunt Question on Everyone's Mind. Available at www.slate.com/articles/health_and_science/science/2012/12/is_earth_f_ked_at_2012_agu_meeting_scientists_consider_advocacy_activism.single.html

Monahan, R., Lesser, B., & Kolodner, M. (2010, July 28). New York City Test Scores Plummet Year After Officials Make Statewide Exams Tougher. *New York Daily News.* Available at articles.nydailynews.com/2010-07-28/local/27071055_1_state-math-tests-test-scores-exams

National Commission on Excellence in Education. (1983). *A nation at risk: The imperative for educational reform: A report to the nation and the Secretary of Education, United States Department of Education.* Washington, DC: Government Printing Office. Available at datacenter.spps.org/uploads/sotw_a_nation_at_risk_1983.pdf

Pauken, T. (2013, January 23). Texas vs. No Child Left Behind. *The American Conservative.* Available at www.theamericanconservative.com/articles/texas-vs-no-child-left-behind/

Porter, E. (2013, April 2). Investments in Education May Be Misdirected. *New York Times.* Available at www.nytimes.com/2013/04/03/business/studies-highlight-benefits-of-early-education.html?_r=0

Primary Sources. (2012). Available at www.scholastic.com/primarysources/pdfs/Gates2012_full.pdf

Ravitch, D. (2011, January 13). The Myth of Charter Schools. *The New York Review of Books.* Available at www.nybooks.com/articles/archives/2010/nov/11/myth-charterschools/?pagination=false

Ravitch, D. (2012, August 9). My View: Rhee Is Wrong and Misinformed. Available at schoolsofthought.blogs.cnn.com/2012/08/09/my-view-rhee-is-wrong-and-misinformed/

Resmovitz, J. (2012, March 21). Teachers' Satisfaction Tanks on Survey When Higher Expectations Come with Fewer Resources. Available at www.huffingtonpost.com/2012/03/21/teachers-dissatisfaction-fewer-resources_n_1365688.html.

Roberts, G. (2012, February 26). Queens Parents Demand Answers Following Teacher's Low Grades. *New York Post.* Available at www.nypost.com/p/news/local/cursed_with_the_worst_in_queens_f5wLhEdDRN1Wl9h1GQgxAM

Royal, C. (2012, November 13). Camika Royal Responds to Critics. Available at dianeravitch.net/?s=camika

Rothstein, R. (2008, April 7). "A Nation at Risk" Twenty-Five Years Later. *CATO Unbound.* Available at www.cato-unbound.org/2008/04/07/richard-rothstein/a-nation-at-risk-twenty-five-years-later/

Rothstein, R., Ladd, H. F., Ravitch, D., Baker, E. L., Barton, P. E., Darling-Hammond, L., Haertel, E., Linn, R. L., Shavelson, R. J., & Shepard, L. A. (2010, August 27). Problems with the Use of Student Test Scores to Evaluate Teachers. Available at www.epi.org/publication/bp278/

Rubinstein, G. (2011, December 1). Miracle Schools: Where Are They Now? Available at garyrubinstein.teachforus.org/2011/12/01/miracle-schools-where-are-they-now/

Scarborough, J. (2012, November 20). My (Semi) Apology to Nate Silver. Available at www.politico.com/news/stories/1112/84115.html

Scharrer, G. (2011, January 16). Ex-Comptroller Strayhorn Finds Vindication in Budget Shortfall. *Houston Chronicle.* Available at www.chron.com/news/houston-texas/article/Ex-comptroller-Strayhorn-finds-vindication-in-1690514.php

School Leadership Briefing. (2011). May 2011 Executive Briefing. Dr. David Berliner: *The Manufactured Crisis* Revisited. Available at www.schoolbriefing.com/1967/the-manufactured-crisis-revisited/

Schuessler, J. (2012, July 16). And the Worst Book of History Is . . . *New York Times.* Available at artsbeat.blogs.nytimes.com/2012/07/16/and-the-worst-book-of-history-is/

Sink, J. (2013, February 14). Obama Campaigns for Universal Pre-K. Available at thehill.com/homenews/administration/283217-obama-campaigns-for-universal-pre-k-education

Sirota, D. (2013, March 11). Getting Rich Off of Schoolchildren. Available at www.salon. com/2013/03/11/getting_rich_off_of_schoolchildren/

Smith, M. (2012a, January 27). Silencing Cheers, to Save Troubled School District. *The New York Times*. Available at www.nytimes.com/2012/01/27/education/premont-tex-schools-suspend-sports-to-save-costs.html?pagewanted=all&_r=0

Smith, M. (2012b, February 2). Scott vs. the World. Available at www.texastribune.org/ texas-education/public-education/scott-vs-world/

Stanford, J. (2013, April 3). Update: Why Did Williams Lie to the Texas Senate? Available at jasonstanford.org/2013/04/why-did-williams-lie-to-the-texas-senate/

Stossel, J. (2006a, January 13). John Stossel's "Stupid in America." Available at abcnews. go.com/2020/Stossel/story?id=1500338

Stossel, J. (2006b, January 13). Stupid in America: Why Your Kids Are Probably Dumber Than Belgians. Available at reason.com/archives/2006/01/13/stupid-in-america

Strauss, V. (2011, May 9). Leading Mathematician Debunks "Value-Added." *Washington Post*. Available at www.washingtonpost.com/blogs/answer-sheet/post/leading-mathematician-debunks-value-added/2011/05/08/AFb999UG_blog.html

Texas Won't Find a Good School Funding System This Way. (2011, March 29). Available at texasedequity.blogspot.com/2011/04/texas-wont-find-good-school-funding.html

Thompson, J. (2011, August 24). Steve Brill's Destructive Morality Play. *Huffington Post*. Available at www.huffingtonpost.com/john-thompson/steve-brill-class-warfare_b_932291.html

Toppo, G. (2008, August 1). "Nation at Risk": The Best or the Worst Thing for Education? *USA Today*. Available at www.usatoday.com/news/education/2008-04-22-nation-at-risk_N.htm

Toyosaburo Korematsu v. United States. 323 U.S. 214. (1944). Available at caselaw. lp.findlaw.com/scripts/getcase.pl?court=US&vol=323&invol=214#fff1.

Transcript of George W. Bush's Acceptance Speech. (n.d.) Available at abcnews.go.com/ Politics/story?id=123214&page=3

The Truth About WWII Internment. (2011, May 27). *Los Angeles Times*. Available at articles.latimes.com/2011/may/27/opinion/la-ed-internment-20110527

Viadero, D. (2009, June 23). Princeton Study Takes Aim at "Value-Added" Measure. *Education Week*. Available at blogs.edweek.org/edweek/inside-schoolresearch/ 2009/06/princeton_study_takes_aim_at_v.html.

Von Radowitz, J. (2012, July 4). Large Hadron Collider Scientists Claim Higgs Boson God Particle Find. *Belfast Telegraph*. Available at www.belfasttelegraph.co.uk /news/world-news/large-hadron-collider-scientists-claim-higgs-boson-god-particle-find-28767564.html

Walton, D. (2000). *Scare tactics: Arguments that appeal to fear and threats*. The Netherlands: Kluwer Academic Publishers.

Weiss, J. (2011, March 31). The Innovation Mismatch: "Smart Capital" and Education Innovation. *Harvard Business Review*. Available at blogs.hbr.org/innovations-in-education/2011/03/the-innovation-mismatch-smart.html

Weiss, J. (2012, November 28). Former Texas Education Commissioner Robert Scott Sparked National Revolt Against High-Stakes Testing. *The Dallas Morning News*. Available at www.dallasnews.com/news/education/headlines/20121128-former-tex-texas-education-commissioner-robert-scott-sparked-national-revolt-against-high-stakes-testing.ece

Winerip, M. (2003, Fall). Houston's "Zero Dropout." Available at www.rethinking-schools.org/special_reports/bushplan/drop181.shtml

Index

✪ ✪ ✪

About the Author

John Kuhn is a public school administrator in Texas. He became a vocal advocate for public education in 2011 when Texas officials enacted unprecedented school-funding cuts while simultaneously embracing the nation's most draconian school accountability system. His "Alamo Letter" and YouTube videos of his 2011 speech at a Save Texas Schools rally went viral, as did his 2012 essay "The Exhaustion of the American Teacher," which garnered over 149,000 "likes" on Facebook. John's other book about education reform, titled *Test-and-Punish*, is forthcoming from Park Place Publications. John is married with three amazing children.